Secrets *of an* English Country House

JULIE MONTAGU
Countess *of* Sandwich

Secrets *of an* English Country House

A YEAR AT MAPPERTON

FRANCES
LINCOLN

CONTENTS

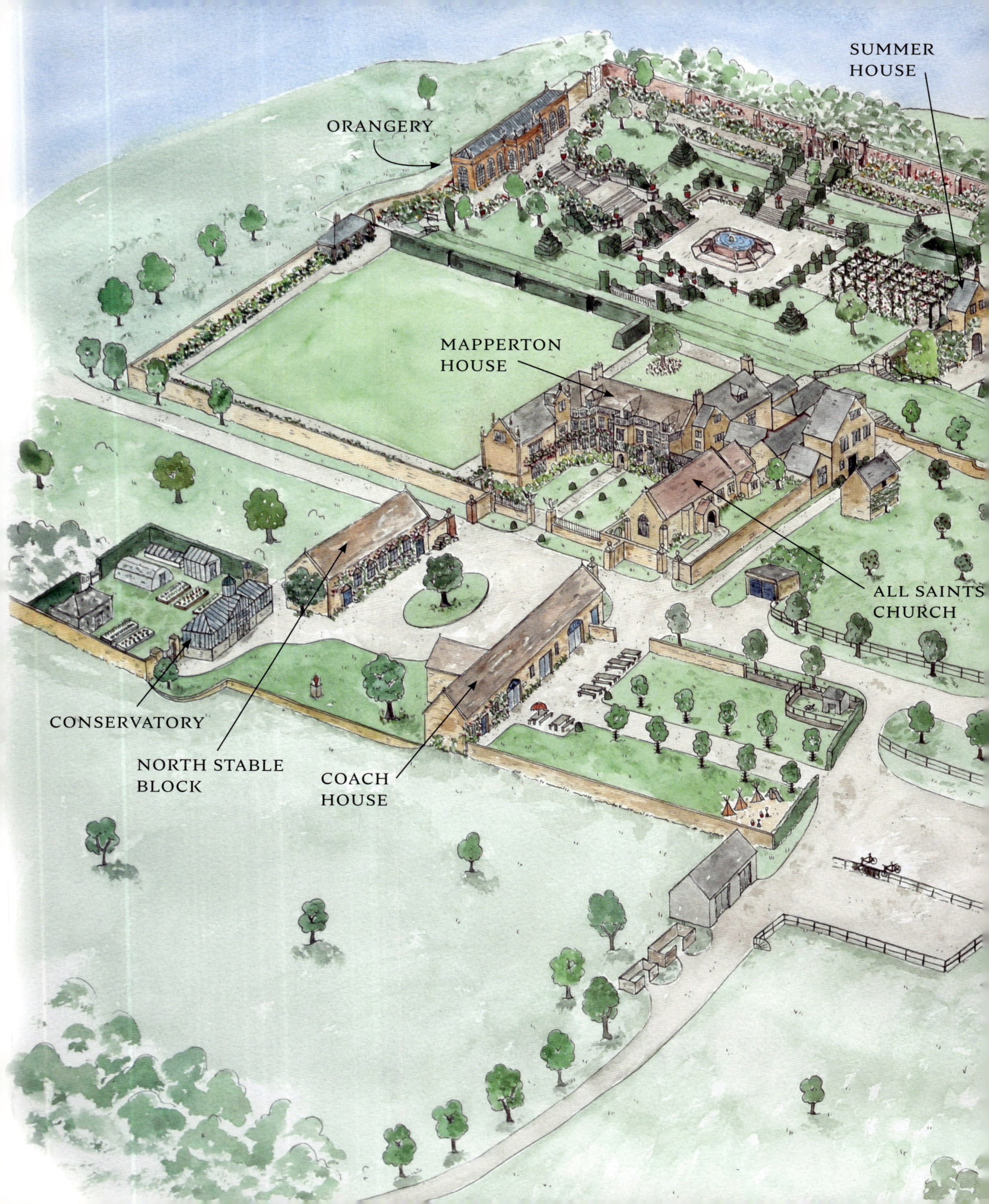
SUMMER HOUSE
ORANGERY
MAPPERTON HOUSE
ALL SAINTS CHURCH
CONSERVATORY
NORTH STABLE BLOCK
COACH HOUSE

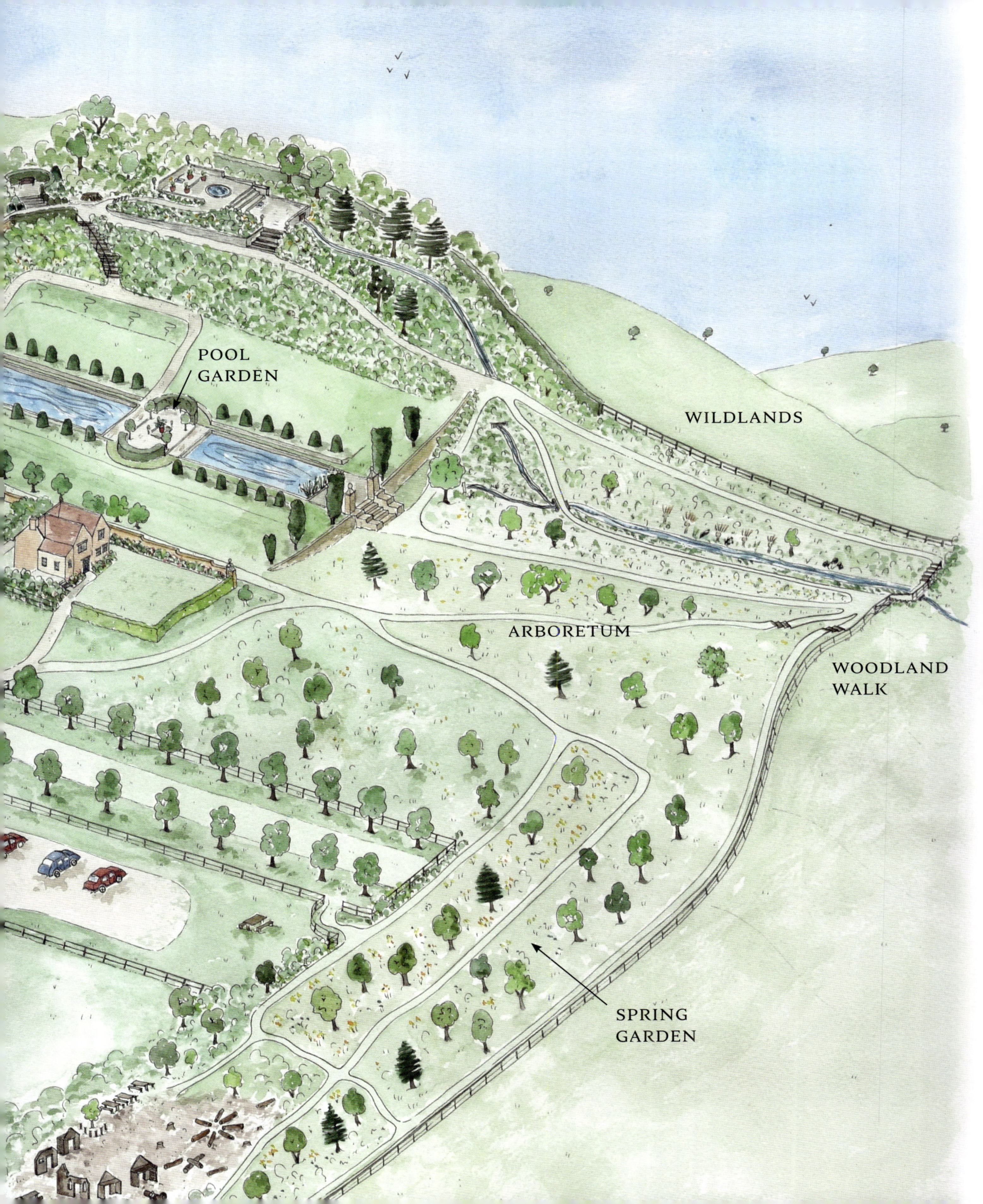
POOL GARDEN
WILDLANDS
ARBORETUM
WOODLAND WALK
SPRING GARDEN

Introduction

The Changing Life of an English Country House

THIS IS NOT A BOOK just about a house – though Mapperton is, I believe, one of the most remarkable surviving manor houses in England. It is a book about a way of life that has had to change, adapt and sometimes be reinvented, generation after generation.

The great English country house was never static. Built to display power, influence or sheer survival, these houses have long mirrored the aspirations – and anxieties – of the families who lived in them. Over time, fortunes rise and fall. Titles pass down, but so too do crumbling roofs, aging paintings and generations of responsibility. We think of these places as timeless, yet they are anything but. Mapperton, like so many houses of its kind, has seen centuries of upheaval – wars, reformations, bankruptcies, destruction, reinvention. What it meant to be the Earl of Sandwich in 1660 is not what it means today. The duties that once defined the aristocracy – managing tenants, maintaining land, serving in Parliament – have slowly been replaced by other imperatives: conservation, public engagement, environmental responsibility and, let's be honest, entrepreneurship.

Country houses are expensive to run. That is a fact. And increasingly, their survival depends not on privilege but on innovation. Weddings in the gardens. Rewilding projects in the valley. Historical tours in the manor. YouTube videos filmed on an iPhone. Today, as the Countess of Sandwich, I find myself as much a content creator, archivist, tour guide, fundraiser and cafe operator as I am a custodian of a centuries-old legacy. And I'm not alone. Across Britain, others in similar roles are doing everything they can to keep these remarkable places alive – not just for their families, but for the wider public.

This book follows the seasons at Mapperton, and with them, the rhythms of life in an English country house. Each chapter explores a different part of the estate and reflects on the people who have shaped them: from Tudor stonemasons to American heiresses, idealistic gardeners to determined modern-day conservators. It's a book about beauty, but also about work. About change, and continuity. About living not in the past, but with the past – and trying to ensure that it has a future.

Julie

A Manor for All Seasons

THE FIRST TIME I CAME TO MAPPERTON, I honestly didn't know what to expect. Luke simply told me that we would be staying at his family home in West Dorset. He described it as 'quite a large house'. I'm American – we're used to big houses. Drive through Connecticut or California and you'll find plenty of them. So I thought, 'All right, I can handle this.'

But as we drove up the narrow lane and Mapperton slowly emerged from behind the trees, I realized this wasn't just a big house – this was a house that had weathered centuries. A house built in the Tudor period, long before the United States had even been founded.

The front of the house, with its honey-coloured Ham stone, feels like something out of a Thomas Hardy novel. And yet it's so real, so solid. When you step inside, the first room you come into is the Hall – and what a hall it is. There's a carved overmantel that immediately draws your eye, dark panelling, creaking floors, an Arts and Crafts ceiling, and a timeless feeling that something important has just happened.

As you move through the house, you can feel the layers of history – the way each century has left its mark. After the Morgans, who built the core of the house in the mid-sixteenth century, came the Brodrepps – four generations of them, all named Richard! From the early 1600s through to the late eighteenth century, they brought a mix of Jacobean elegance and Georgian refinement to Mapperton. The main staircase, for example – gracefully carved and just grand enough – was the work of the wonderfully named Bastard Brothers of Blandford, renowned local builders. Some of the balusters were even installed upside-down, whether by accident or as a little architectural joke, no one quite knows. And then, in the 1700s, yet another Richard decided to give the house more fashionable flair, adding the rococo ceiling in the Library, full of playful swirls and ornamental flourishes.

One of my favourite rooms is the Drawing Room. Its ceiling is the original Tudor one, dotted with crests from the Brett and Morgan families – lions, fleurs-de-lis – subtle reminders of Mapperton's deep-rooted past. The room has a gentle air of light and calm, and tucked within it is a portrait of Martha Ray, a beautiful singer and the tragic mistress of the 4th Earl of Sandwich. She was murdered outside Covent Garden Theatre by a jealous lover.

Upstairs, the Great Chamber is a marvel. The plaster ceiling – a pendant design from the sixteenth century – is simply extraordinary. Some of the same Flemish motifs you see there also appear in the overmantel in the West Room. It's all part of Mapperton's quiet interconnectedness. Nothing is ever random; every detail feels like it has grown into place.

A Georgian dining table, set within the richly panelled Dining Room.

And then, of course, there's Mrs Ethel Labouchere – the indomitable woman who bought Mapperton in 1919 and gave it a second life. She was the widow of a prominent banker, and she poured her energy into the house. She added ceilings, yes – the wonderful Arts and Crafts ones in the Hall and Dining Room – but she also laid out the foundations of the Italianate gardens. They're one of the reasons people fall in love with Mapperton.

For the house is just one part of it. Mapperton sits in a steep valley surrounded by 750 ha (1,850 acres) of farmland, pasture, woodland and gardens. The Italianate terraces descend from the house in formal layers – symmetrical topiary, gravel paths, fountains and urns – but beyond that, the land becomes wilder. There are old fish ponds (now a spring-fed swimming pool and a lily pond), a small stone summer house and, further still, the start of what we now call the Mapperton Wildlands.

When Luke and I moved here in 2016, we were stepping into a long family history, but also into a house, gardens and estate that needed looking after, and in some areas reimagining. We've opened the house and gardens to visitors eight months of the year, created a cafe and shop in the Coach House, and restored parts of the house and estate buildings that were slowly falling into disrepair. We've built events and exhibitions into the rhythm of the place, helping to support Mapperton as a living, working home.

One of my favourite projects has been the archives. What was once a damp, dark room is now a fully functioning research space. It houses the Montagu family papers and a treasure trove of letters, journals and household documents. I've spent many hours there, often wrapped in a wool scarf and gloves, scanning an Edwardian countess's letters or reading eighteenth-century inventories. It's where the past begins to speak again – quietly, patiently – if you're willing to listen.

In 1955, after Ethel's death, Mapperton was bought by Luke's grandfather Victor Montagu, then Viscount Hinchingbrooke. It's been in the family ever since. The portrait in the Hall of the 1st Earl of Sandwich – a cousin of Samuel Pepys and the man who brought Charles II back from exile – hangs on the panelling Richard Brodrepp installed. The stories run deep here.

Every time I walk through the house – especially when it's quiet – I'm reminded how much of a responsibility and privilege it is to live here. Mapperton has survived and adapted through centuries of war, peace, decline, revival and now conservation. And what I've come to realize is that while the house looks back, it also looks forwards.

This book follows a year in the life of Mapperton: not just the house, but the gardens, the Wildlands and everything in between. You'll find old recipes and archive stories, seasonal changes in the landscape, moments with family, and all the beauty and chaos that come with living in one of England's most remarkable manor houses.

Because despite its history – and perhaps because of it – Mapperton is still evolving. And I'm so looking forward to sharing it with you.

FACING Julie in the Staircase Hall, which is dressed with a seasonal foliage garland wound from the estate. OVERLEAF Wisteria in full bloom cascading across the facade of the north stable block in spring.

900 Years of Mapperton

MAPPERTON'S STORY BEGINS more than 900 years ago. It's recorded in the Domesday Book of 1086 – the great survey commissioned by William the Conqueror – which lists it as 'a modest settlement'. Even then, the land was valuable: nestled in a quiet West Dorset valley, fed by a spring, and probably occupied by a rudimentary manor or smallholding. That deep-rooted continuity – of land, life and care – forms the bedrock of everything that came after.

By the reign of Edward I in the late thirteenth century, Mapperton was associated with the Brett family. It then appears in a 1423 document as *Bryttesmaperton*, a name that ties the place to its lineage and landscape. Over the following six centuries, the estate would remain in the hands of just four principal families – Brett, Morgan, Brodrepp and Compton – passing more than once through the female line. Country houses have often relied not just on titles, but on daughters, nieces and strategic marriages to survive.

The house as we know it today was largely shaped in the mid-sixteenth century by Robert Morgan, a descendant of the Morgan family who had held Mapperton since the fourteenth century, when the Brett heiress married a Morgan. Robert extended the manor using soft Ham Hill stone from nearby Somerset. He crowned the house with twisted finials topped by heraldic beasts, eccentric and proud. There may well have been a medieval building here before, but the Mapperton that survives today is unmistakably Tudor.

In the seventeenth century, the estate passed once again through marriage, this time into the Brodrepp family. Richard Brodrepp II added much of what defines Mapperton today: the oak panelling in the Hall, the remodelled west front, the stable blocks and the rebuilt nave of All Saints Church, still just a few steps from the house.

After more than six centuries of inheritance, Mapperton was finally sold in 1919. The new owner, Mrs Ethel Labouchere, brought her own distinctive aesthetic. The Italianate gardens she commissioned continue to evolve under our care.

When Victor Montagu purchased Mapperton in 1955, Hinchingbrooke House in Huntingdonshire had been home to nine Earls of Sandwich, but they also owned land in West Dorset. Like so many great houses, Hinchingbrooke – the family's principal seat since 1627 – had suffered during the Second World War. It had been requisitioned, fallen into disrepair and become increasingly difficult to maintain. In the early 1960s, the decision was made to sell it. The house was eventually purchased by Huntingdonshire County Council and converted into a comprehensive secondary school – Hinchingbrooke School – which it remains to this day.

The Staircase Hall, lined with ancestral portraits.

Yet the family's connection to Mapperton goes back even further. In 1906, Alberta Sturges – an American heiress, Victor's mother and the last countess to live at Hinchingbrooke – visited Mapperton Court. Writing to her own mother after the visit, she captured its quiet enchantment: 'Never in all my life have I seen a small Elizabethan home so beautiful . . . all old oak and wood panelling . . . diamond panes, creepers outlining every window . . . clematis . . . lavender and honeysuckle.' Even then, Mapperton stood apart: untouched, tucked into the hills, waiting for its next chapter.

Victor inherited the earldom in 1962, becoming the 10th Earl of Sandwich, though he renounced his title two years later in order to remain in the House of Commons. The title passed to my father-in-law, John Montagu, upon the death of Victor in 1995. In the 1980s, John and my mother-in-law, Caroline, moved into Mapperton. They breathed new life into it – restoring, conserving, replanting and adapting the house for modern life while honouring its long history. Mapperton has survived not through preservation alone, but through reinvention.

Today, Luke, my husband, is the 12th Earl of Sandwich, and together we are the most recent generation to care for this remarkable place. Mapperton isn't a museum. It's our home. And like the generations before us, we're doing all we can to ensure it endures.

A pair of giltwood marquises in Régence style, with eighteenth-century Aubusson tapestry upholstery, shell-carved cabriole legs and pad feet.

Family Tree

William the Conqueror (1028–87) m. Matilda of Flanders (1031–83)

Henry I of England (1068–1135) m. Matilda of Scotland (1080–1118)

Geoffrey Plantagenet (1113–51) m. Empress Matilda (1102–67)

Henry II of England (1133–89) m. Eleanor of Aquitaine (1122–1204)

King John (1166–1216) m. Isabella of Angoulême (1186–1246)

Henry III of England (1207–72) m. Eleanor of Provence (1223–91)

Edward I of England (1239–1307) m. Eleanor of Castile (1241–90)

Ralph de Monthermer (1270–1325) m. Joan of Acre (1272–1307)

Thomas de Monthermer (1301–40) m. Margaret de Brewes (1307–49)

John de Montagu (1330–90) m. Margaret Monthermer (1329–93)

Sir Simon Montagu (1353–?) m. Elizabeth Montagu (1353–?)

Thomas Montagu (1375–99) m. Christina Basser (1377–1477)

John Montagu (1397–1419) m. Alice Holcot (1399–1431)

Sir William Montagu (?–1455) m. Margaret Bullen (1426–1520)

Thomas Montagu of Hemington (1452–1517) m. Agnes Dudley (1454–1501)

Edward Montagu (1485–1557) m. Elenor Roper (1500–63)

Edward Montagu of Boughton (1530–1602) — m. Elizabeth Harrington (1545–1618)

Sir Sidney Montagu (1581–1644) — m. Paulina Pepys (1581–1641)

Edward Montagu, 1st Earl of Sandwich (1625–72) — m. Jemima Crew (1625–74)

Edward Montagu, 2nd Earl of Sandwich (1648–88) — m. Lady Anne Boyle (1625–71)

Edward Montagu, 3rd Earl of Sandwich (1670–1729) — m. Elizabeth of Wilmot (1674–1757)

Edward Montagu, Viscount Hinchingbrooke (1692–1722) — m. Elizabeth Popham (1693–1761)

John Montagu, 4th Earl of Sandwich (1744–1814) — m. Lady Mary Paulet (?–1779)

George Montagu 5th Earl of Sandwich (1773–1819) — m. Lady Louisa Lowry–Corry (1781–1862)

John Montagu, 7th Earl of Sandwich (1811–84) — m. Lady Mary Paget (1812–59)

Victor Alexander Montagu (1841–1915) — m. Lady Agneta Harriet (1838–1913)

George Montagu, 9th Earl of Sandwich (1874–1902) — m. Alberta Sturges (1877–1951)

Victor Montagu, 10th Earl of Sandwich (1906–95) — m. Maud Rosemary Peto (1916–98)

John Montagu, 11th Earl of Sandwich (1943–2025) — m. Caroline Hayman

Luke Montagu, 12th Earl of Sandwich — m. Julie Fisher

William Montagu, Viscount Hinchingbrooke

Mapperton and Hinchingbrooke House Timeline

MAPPERTON HOUSE — KEY DATES

1086
Mapperton recorded in the Domesday Book

13TH–15TH CENTURIES
Held by the **Brett family**
Recorded as Bryttesmaperton (1423)

16TH CENTURY
Morgan family extended the house beyond the medieval core

17TH–18TH CENTURIES
Brodrepp family inherit by marriage

1774–1919
Compton family ownership
House passes through the female line

1919
Mapperton sold out of the family for the first time in six centuries

1919–1955
Owned by **Mrs Ethel Labouchere**

1955
Purchased by **Victor Montagu**, Viscount Hinchingbrooke
Mapperton becomes the new family seat

HICHINGBROOKE HOUSE — KEY DATES

C.1100

Norman church built on the site, thought to replace an older Saxon church

C.1200

Benedictine nunnery established on the site

Functions as a religious house until the Dissolution

1536

Dissolution of the Monasteries, including Hinchingbrooke Nunnery

Nunnery lands acquired by the Crown

1538

Granted to the Cromwell family (at a favourable rate, as with many former monastic properties)

1627

Purchased from the Cromwells by **Sir Sidney Montagu**

Son **Edward Montagu** is aged two

1660

Edward Montagu instrumental in the Restoration

Created 1st Earl of Sandwich by Charles II

17TH–20TH CENTURIES

Hinchingbrooke House remains the principal family seat

Home to nine successive Earls of Sandwich

EARLY 20TH CENTURY

Residence of **George Montagu** and **Alberta Sturges Montagu, 9th Earl and Countess**

Last Earl and Countess of Sandwich to live at Hinchingbrooke

1955

Their son **Victor Montagu** leaves Hinchingbrooke as his primary residence

Purchases Mapperton House in Dorset

Spring

THERE IS A MOMENT – usually in late March or early April – when Mapperton seems to exhale. And there's that peculiar mix of damp soil and blossom that means everything is about to begin again.

Spring at Mapperton is not the manicured season of Palladian estates with rows of forced tulips. It is, rather, one of gentle reclamation. The wild comes knocking at our door again, spilling into the garden and land with cow parsley, fleabane, wild garlic and bluebells leading the charge.

It's the light, too. That soft Dorset light that begins to stretch past five o'clock, revealing how much there is to do. After months of closed doors and dark corners, spring is when Mapperton starts to come alive again.

It is the season when the rhythms of the manor house shift from hibernation to hospitality. Mapperton in springtime feels kinetic. There is a joy in it, yes, but also a restlessness. We are never more aware of time than when the clock is restarting.

My mother-in-law has always said that if Mapperton had no house at all, people would still come for the gardens. In spring, they transform into a kind of theatre of movement: the swaying of daffodils and tulips, the steady growth of grasses, seedlings and, of course, the glorious wisteria in the garden; the bluebells, wild garlic and hum of returning pollinators in the Wildlands. It is a place where old and new horticultural philosophies meet – where structure and wildness are allowed to coexist. Over the past decade, we've become more intentional in how we interact with the landscape, letting the natural rhythms of rewilding shape our stewardship. And yet paths are still swept, the borders edged, the heritage roses pruned.

Spring is also the season when the public returns. Mapperton, which might feel like a private world in the depths of winter, opens again to visitors. Curious minds, garden enthusiasts, and families in search of fresh air and English history arrive – often clutching a map or just following the scent of coffee and cake to the Coach House cafe. Behind the scenes, of course, it's a sprint. Repairs are made in the nick of time, flower beds are raked and edged, signage is refreshed and tearoom menus are quietly adjusted – with sandwiches, naturally, taking pride of place. We are, after all, the Sandwich family.

It's a time when Mapperton feels busiest and brightest. Our volunteers are back, offering warm welcomes and leading house tours that bring history to life in every room. Others are out in the Wildlands, helping to monitor the Exmoor ponies, maintain the

West-facing front elevation of the house with clematis in bloom.

rewilding trails, or support the garden team as they prepare for our growing season. What we're building here is something bigger than a private estate – it's a shared story. Heritage, after all, isn't something to hoard. It's something to pass on.

As I walk through the house in early spring, I'm always struck by the contrast between indoors and out. The walls of the Tudor manor still hold the cool of winter, but the windows begin to glow. This is where the story begins: with Robert Morgan and his wife Mary, who built the house in the mid-sixteenth century. There are whispers of them still – in the stone, the ceilings, the overmantel in the Hall. It's remarkable to think that generations have lived and worked here for more than five hundred years, each adding and removing, adapting the house to their own needs.

Mapperton doesn't reinvent itself each spring. It simply resumes. The house, the gardens, the land – they don't ask to be noticed. But they reward those who do. There's something reassuring in that return, in the knowledge that even after the longest winter, this place always finds its way back to life.

As they say in Italy, *la primavera bussa dolcemente alla porta* – spring knocks gently at the door.

Cow parsley in full spring growth along the upper bank beside the summer house.

ABOVE *(left)* A sundial positioned at the top of the Fountain Court steps. *(right)* Geraniums carefully arranged and tended inside the conservatory. OVERLEAF The conservatory in full spring bloom, with vibrant planting framed by the Coach House beyond.

Tudor Origins

WHEN PEOPLE ASK ME which is my favourite season at Mapperton, I never quite know how to answer – each one reveals a different facet of the house. But spring is when the light creeps into corners that have long been shadowed, and in one such corner, hidden behind the Drawing Room panelling, is a secret that I must share.

It's a long-lost Tudor door.

Not the current entrance on the west side – this one is tucked away, out of sight, concealed behind carefully fitted wood panelling. It dates to the sixteenth century and would once have opened directly out on to the grounds. What lay beyond it, we can't say for certain. But the fact that it remains – still in place after all these centuries – feels like a rare and unexpected survival.

This is one of my favourite moments on house tours – I gently open the panel and reveal the stone frame. The reactions are always the same: gasps, then silence, then questions. There's something quietly thrilling about revealing a piece of the house that appears entirely hidden, as though the building itself is letting you in on a secret. We don't include the Tudor door on the official house tours – not because I don't want people to see it, but because it's a rather fiddly business. But when I'm leading the tour myself, I make sure to show it. And that moment – that slow reveal – is always worth the trouble.

I like to think of Robert Morgan stepping through that door in the 1540s, fresh from overseeing work on the north wing, its corner pilasters capped with his heraldic beasts bearing shields of arms – a clear display of lineage and pride. Morgan, who married Mary Wogan, had inherited Mapperton through his Brett ancestors. And it's important to remember that this wasn't just a period of local building. The 1540s were the aftermath of one of the most dramatic upheavals in English history: the Dissolution of the Monasteries. Under Henry VIII, vast monastic estates were seized, redistributed and reimagined.

Mapperton wasn't part of that great ecclesiastical purge, but Morgan was building in a landscape irrevocably changed by it. As the old religious houses fell into ruin, new manorial identities were quite literally being built up stone by stone. It's tempting to think that Morgan, like many gentry of the time, saw this as an opportunity – a moment to solidify status, to anchor his family more firmly in the shifting world Henry had left in his wake. Mapperton, in that sense, is a Tudor house born of both continuity and disruption.

You can still see the traces of Morgan's heritage throughout the house. The Brett lion and the Morgan fleur-de-lis in the Tudor ceiling of the Drawing Room – their emblems remain.

A sixteenth-century stone archway and enclave within the Hall.

Dr Tim Connor, an architectural historian, has written about this period of construction with careful detail. He records an inscription that was noted in 1774 as being in the Hall, crediting Robert Morgan and Mary his wife with building the house at their own charge and cost, and ending with the lines: 'What they spent, that they lent; what they gave, that they have; what they left, that they lost.' Although the inscription is no longer visible today, Connor suggests it may survive behind the great chimneypiece installed in the Hall in 1909. What a sentiment. It's so very Tudor: pious and pragmatic, proud and restrained. Robert Morgan built the Hall, that door and most of the north wing, perhaps not in one sweep, but steadily, purposefully and likely with the idea of permanence. And yet nothing is ever truly permanent in a house like this.

By the time the Brodrepp family took ownership in the early seventeenth century (by marriage again – a recurring theme in Mapperton's lineage), the house had already started to shift its orientation. Richard Brodrepp II began remodelling the west front – the side of the house that faces today's drive. It was during this time that things migrated, literally turning the house around. My favourite Tudor door became an interior relic, but, blessedly, it was just covered over, which is why we can still open that panel in the Drawing Room and time-travel straight into the sixteenth century.

These hidden traces of Mapperton's Tudor past don't end with the door. Upstairs, the Great Chamber retains one of the finest sixteenth-century pendant plaster ceilings in any domestic setting in England. It is breathtaking – and not just because of its beauty.

In an historic English house, the Great Chamber was the lord's private reception room: a space of prestige and control located above the more public Great Hall. It offered some measure of privacy from the bustle of the household below, and served as a formal sitting room and reception area for honoured guests. In the hierarchy of rooms, it was second in importance only to the Great Hall itself – a powerful architectural signal of wealth, taste and status.

And Mapperton's ceiling rises to that occasion. Its design, with hanging pendants, ribbed compartments and stylized floral bosses, places

ABOVE The original north-facing Tudor door, one of the oldest surviving features of the house. FACING (*top*) Intricate fleur-de-lis motifs carved into the ornate Drawing Room ceiling. (*bottom*) The Drawing Room interior. OVERLEAF The west front of Mapperton, with All Saints Church attached to the house.

the house within a circle of elite Tudor interiors influenced by the architectural fashions of Henry VIII's court. It's easy to forget, standing beneath it in rural West Dorset, that these forms – these delicate pendants suspended from ribbed plaster panels – were once the very image of royal grandeur. They echoed the ceilings at Hampton Court and Nonsuch Palace (demolished in the 1680s), both of which helped to set the decorative tone for noble and gentry houses in the 1540s and 1550s.

What makes Mapperton's ceiling even more remarkable is its striking resemblance to the pendant ceiling in the Great Chamber at Gilling Castle in North Yorkshire – a design dated to 1585. Architectural historians suggest both were likely drawn from the same pattern book or executed by craftsmen working to similar specifications. As *Some Dorset Manor Houses* (1907) notes, the ceiling of the Great Chamber places Mapperton within a broader national network of Tudor decorative fashion, showing that even in the far reaches of West Dorset, the visual language of courtly interiors was being fluently spoken.

Within the cornice are profile heads – male and female – whose stylized faces also appear on the overmantel in the West Bedroom. They may share a source with carved wooden medallions found in places like St Cross, Winchester, or be part of a Continental motif circulating through emblem books at the time. Their presence gives the ceiling a sense of theatre and symbolism.

I often stand beneath that ceiling and wonder if Robert Morgan ever looked up at it with pride, realizing he had brought something truly regal to his Dorset manor. It's one thing to build with stone and lineage, another to crown your chamber with a ceiling once reserved for kings.

There's something about spring that brings those Tudor bones of the house back to life. I imagine the builders, the masons, the carvers, even Robert Morgan himself, measuring angles, placing beasts atop parapets, and laying the first foundation stones for a house that would stand – and evolve – for nearly five centuries.

FACING The west-facing entrance to the house, approached through the front courtyard. ABOVE Cleaning the Tudor overmantel in the West Bedroom as part of Mapperton's ongoing conservation work.

I often wonder what that Tudor door once opened on to. It clearly led out to the grounds, but what those grounds looked like in the sixteenth century remains a mystery. Perhaps there was a courtyard or an open space, perhaps something more structured. We simply don't know. But like the door itself, it hints at an earlier rhythm of life – one that has shifted, evolved and in some ways disappeared.

Every time I open that panel, I think of all the thresholds Mapperton has crossed. From medieval manor to Tudor estate, from Restoration-era remodelling to Georgian refinement, from Edwardian revival to post-war adaptation. And now, in our own time, a layered, living home – full of stories, secrets and the occasional hidden door waiting to be rediscovered.

So if you're on my tour, I'll show you what lies behind the panel. But I warn you – once you see that Tudor door, once you stand there imagining what it once looked out upon, you'll never walk through Mapperton in quite the same way again.

ABOVE The ornate pendant plaster ceiling of the Great Chamber, a masterpiece of decorative craftsmanship. FACING The interior of the Great Chamber, conveying its impressive scale and richly decorated plasterwork.

A Garden in Memory

SPRING AT MAPPERTON announces itself with a crescendo of colour and scent, coaxing the estate out of its winter quiet. It is a season of new beginnings, and fittingly that is also where our garden story starts – with Mapperton's transformation into a horticultural haven under the visionary eye of its new owner.

When Mrs Ethel Labouchere bought Mapperton in 1919, the estate had just passed out of the same family line for the first time in six centuries. The First World War had ended. The country was reeling. Widowed and in search of a project both personal and purposeful, Ethel made the brave and visionary decision to create something entirely new: a garden to honour the memory of her husband, Charles Henry Labouchere, a Dutch banker. Between 1920 and 1927, she commissioned and oversaw the creation of what would become the bones of Mapperton's 6-ha (15-acre) formal garden.

There is substantial evidence to suggest that a Dorset architect, Charles William Pike, designed the gardens, possibly drawing inspiration from the leading landscape architect and garden designer of the day, Harold Peto. His design was strongly geometric and Italianate in conception, developed within the existing framework of an earlier garden.

Ethel's creation begins at the Fountain Court, where symmetry and serenity reign. Here, a quiet rectangular space is framed by orderly quadrants of clipped box and statuary. At the centre of it all is a pool, its waters gently stirred by a central fountain.

Yet Ethel's ambition extended far beyond the Fountain Court. She commissioned a pair of Italianate grottos – magical enclaves carved into the hillside. Built into the embankments that shape Mapperton's hidden valleys, the grottos feel both mysterious and ancient.

Very little information survives about the detailed planting of this early period. No contemporary photographs exist of Ethel's garden, though images from the mid- to late 1950s – just before Victor Montagu began his alterations – provide some sense of its appearance. Surviving garden records kept after 1955 suggest that the majority of the planting in Fountain Court, apart from the topiary, consisted largely of roses, supplemented with colourful annuals and flowering perennials.

One of Ethel Labouchere's great gifts to Mapperton is that she worked with the landscape, not against it. The steeply terraced layout is not only a feat of design, but also a quiet act of humility – an acknowledgement

FACING The Fountain Court arranged with geometric quadrants and neatly clipped planting beds. OVERLEAF The terraced Italianate gardens, dramatically structured across the natural contours of the valley.

of the contours of the land. The Italianate terraces draw the visitor downwards, gently encouraging a pilgrimage through different moods and elevations.

And here, too, she gave Mapperton one of its most touching gestures: two plaques, discreetly placed, dedicated to the memory of Charles Henry Labouchere and to the workers who brought the gardens to life.

Her work, however, was not intended to end with her lifetime. The structure she laid down – the terracing, the formal areas, the framing grottos – provided the bones for future generations to flesh out. That's the enduring magic of the gardens: they are simultaneously of their time and yet somehow timeless. They've been reshaped, nurtured and extended, but they always return to Ethel's vision, season after season.

It's often said that gardening is the slowest of the performing arts. If so, Mrs Labouchere was a master choreographer. What she composed at Mapperton continues to unfold every spring, with each blossom and unfurling leaf, each new visitor pausing in quiet wonder.

Today, when visitors walk through Mapperton in the spring, they may not know Ethel's name, but they feel her hand in everything, for her garden invites contemplation – not only of nature, but of time, and of the love that planted it.

ABOVE (*left*) Memorial plaque to Charles Henry Labouchere, in whose memory the Italianate gardens were created. (*right*) Plaque commemorating the gardeners and estate workers who created the Italianate gardens. FACING A stone owl nestled within shaded topiary in the gardens.

FACING The grotto, a picturesque feature associated with Mrs Labouchere's tenure at Mapperton.

ABOVE The coat of arms of Mrs Labouchere displayed in the Entrance Hall. OVERLEAF Terraced Italianate gardens descending through the valley at Mapperton.

Luke Montagu

EARL OF SANDWICH

Running Mapperton as a working estate, family home and visitor destination is very much a team effort, and at the centre of that team is my husband, Luke. Together we've faced a global pandemic, leaking roofs and more than one water emergency the day before a wedding. Since stepping into our roles ten years ago, we've navigated both the traditional responsibilities of historic house life and some very modern challenges – including launching a YouTube channel that now reaches viewers around the world. In this conversation, Luke looks back on how Mapperton has adapted, survived and evolved – not just for us, but for the next generation.

JULIE Luke, we've now been working together at Mapperton for a decade. In that time, we've done many of the traditional things historic houses do – opening to the public, hosting weddings and stewarding these extraordinary but often temperamental old buildings. But in 2020, we did something rather unexpected: we launched a YouTube channel. What was that like for you?

LUKE Honestly? It started in a moment of panic. When the pandemic hit, we lost all our visitor income overnight. No cafe, no house tours, no events. And yet, of course, all the expenses were still there – the gardens still needed tending, the roof still leaked and we had a team to support. It was a pretty unsettling time.

But what we realized was that although people couldn't visit Mapperton in person, we could bring Mapperton to them. You had your background in presenting, I had mine in film and digital media – and between us, we had a smartphone, a very long Internet cable and a slightly naive belief it might just work.

JULIE I still remember our first livestream. Your parents were in the church, I was in front of the camera and you were trailing behind as cameraman; Nestor, age thirteen, was the soundman.

LUKE And we had no Wi-Fi in the church, so we ran a cable across the gravel, through the gate, and prayed it wouldn't cut out mid-sentence. It was chaotic, but oddly magical. Hundreds of people joined, many from North America. They were commenting live, asking questions and even donating. I'll never forget when my mother turned to the camera and said, 'We need to fix the church tower. Any volunteers?' And within forty-eight hours, we'd raised over £1,000. That was the moment we realized something important was happening.

JULIE Mapperton was reaching beyond its walls.

LUKE Exactly. And from there, it snowballed. We applied for funding from the government's Culture Recovery Fund. We got proper equipment, hired a team to help – and 'Mapperton Live!' launched officially in 2021. One of our early videos – you pressure-washing the eighteenth-century pool – went viral, and the channel just grew from there.

JULIE I still don't quite understand why that video resonated!

LUKE Something about you, in wellies, with a pressure washer. The Internet loved it.

JULIE And we saw a real-world impact. People started coming to Mapperton after discovering it online. Some flew from the US just to visit.

LUKE It was the beginning of a kind of digital renaissance for the estate. And it didn't stop with YouTube – it led to everything from our Patreon community to fundraising campaigns, Grand Historic Tours and even the Alberta Research Project (see page 222).

JULIE Let's go back a bit, though. Before YouTube, before livestreaming – what was it like when we first took on the running of Mapperton?

LUKE I remember sitting down with the accounts in 2015 and thinking: 'This isn't sustainable.' The estate was running at a loss, and had been for some time. So we began by focusing on the fundamentals: increasing income and reducing costs through improving our existing activities. We converted the south stable block into a cafe and events space. That allowed us to host weddings and increase visitor numbers. Then came the new drive, car park, proper loos; five-star lavatories are non-negotiable.

JULIE And we tried glamping.

LUKE Yes – until two of the bell tents blew away in a summer storm. That was disheartening. But it's something we may revisit. We also began converting some of the estate cottages into holiday lets. It's always a balance – we want a vibrant, lived-in estate, but letting out a few cottages helps generate critical income.

JULIE And now that the infrastructure is in place, what does your average week actually look like?

LUKE Oh goodness. Where do I begin? I wear many hats. Marketing for the weddings and holiday lets – each of those is its own mini-business. Then there's compliance, risk assessments, health and safety. I also double as IT manager – usually found crouched under a desk trying to coax a router back to life. There's also the day-to-day maintenance: leaks, gutters, broken gates, fallen trees. And, of course, managing our wonderful team, making sure everyone's aligned.

JULIE And we film two videos a week on top of all that.

LUKE Yes. It's a lot. 'Spilling the Tea' (our monthly news update) has become its own little phenomenon. But it does require constant creativity. You wake up thinking, 'What can we film today?' And sometimes, you're just not in the mood to be cheerful on camera. But the funny thing is, the act of filming often lifts our spirits.

JULIE Even when the reservoir has emptied itself. Again.

LUKE Oh yes. The reservoir. We've lost count of how many times a leaking pipe somewhere on the estate has drained the entire thing – usually the day before a wedding.

JULIE Which has meant, more than once, placing a last-minute emergency order for luxury portaloos.

LUKE I've spent far too many evenings panicking over our water supply. Water is non-negotiable.

JULIE But those are the stories people don't always hear – the behind-the-scenes chaos, the resilience it takes to keep everything running.

LUKE Exactly. This isn't just about preserving buildings. It's about keeping a whole ecosystem alive. And some days, it really does feel like holding it together with string and gaffer tape.

JULIE And yet, five years on, Mapperton feels more alive than ever. We even won the inaugural Historic Houses Diversification Award in 2025.

LUKE That was a huge moment. It wasn't just an award for doing something different – it was recognition that we'd made it sustainable. That we'd built something meaningful. Something that could help Mapperton thrive for the future.

JULIE And we're not finished yet. There are still projects we hope to complete before William takes over.

LUKE Absolutely. We'd love to restore two of the farmyards – one as a cluster of holiday cottages, the other potentially as a venue or space for commercial use. They're beautiful buildings, but in need of care.

JULIE Mapperton has always evolved. YouTube is just the latest chapter, and one we never saw coming.

LUKE And now, with all these new connections – online, in person and across the estate – we feel more hopeful than ever that Mapperton will continue to grow, inspire and entertain!

Luke and Julie in the Wildlands with White Park cattle within the rewilding landscape.

A Quiet Revolution During Lockdown

IT BEGAN, AS SO MANY meaningful things do, in silence.

In the spring of 2020, with the world locked down, we found ourselves in an unfamiliar quiet at Mapperton. The gates were shut. The gardens bloomed unseen. There were no visitors wandering the topiary, no conversations echoing across the croquet lawn, no wedding parties arriving in antique cars. Just birdsong, wind in the beech trees and the slowing down of everything.

It was in that pause that the first threads of what would become Mapperton Wildlands began to unfurl – not in a boardroom or on a strategy document, but in our kitchen, our walks, our children's questions. With all of us at home, those long lockdown days opened space for new kinds of conversations. The kind that only happen when there's nowhere to rush off to, and everything to reconsider.

The children had never been comfortable with the shoot. And then, there was *that* moment when our son, at just eleven years old, crept into the pheasant pens and cut the fencing. Not out of mischief, but out of conviction. He wanted to free the birds. And astonishingly, he did. Over the next few days, around a thousand pheasants scattered across the valley seeking escape.

It was shocking. But it was also clarifying. That act – a child's protest – made it impossible to ignore what we already knew deep down: that the old systems – of shooting, of fencing, of managing every corner – no longer fit the world we wanted our children to inherit.

So we asked ourselves a simple but, at the time, rather radical question: what if we stepped back?

That question had been taking shape in our minds for some time, thanks in large part to the extraordinary work at Knepp in West Sussex. Charlie Burrell and Isabella Tree had reimagined their struggling estate as a space for nature to reclaim, introducing free-roaming grazers and stepping back from traditional farming altogether. Their courage to let go – and the astonishing return of wildlife that followed – was not only inspiring, it helped embolden us to ask different questions here at Mapperton. Knepp showed what was possible when you trust natural processes. Their pioneering work was instrumental in shaping our own approach to rewilding, reminding us that hope often begins with humility.

The principles that emerged were deceptively simple. We would minimize intervention. No more rigid land management plans designed to deliver predetermined outcomes. Instead, we would listen to the soil, to the weather, to the creatures. We'd resist the urge to 'improve' or curate. Nature, we realized, doesn't need us to micromanage – it needs us to get out of the way.

Standing deadwood within the Wildlands, retained as habitat for insects, birds and fungi.

We would create connected landscapes. Mapperton is cradled in the heart of West Dorset's valley system, and we knew that isolated patches of wildness weren't enough. We opened gates, tore down internal fences, and looked for opportunities to join our land with that of others. Wildlife corridors, not walled gardens.

We would support natural grazing. That meant introducing free-roaming grazing animals – like our White Park cattle – not to 'mow' the landscape, but to mimic the large herbivores that once shaped Britain's ecosystems. Their hoofprints churn the soil, their dung feeds insects, and their gentle meandering opens up space for scrub, grassland and wild flowers to emerge.

We would make room for water. Mapperton is defined by its flowing valley and part of our rewilding meant rethinking water management. Slowing it. Letting seasonal pools return. Embracing the messy, marshy margins that support frogs, birds and bugs instead of draining them away.

And perhaps most importantly, we would embrace uncertainty. Rewilding isn't tidy. There are no neat outcomes. It's about standing back, watching closely and learning. Some years the butterflies come in abundance. Other years the grass gets ahead of the flowers. But that's the point. It's not about control. It's about letting nature breathe again.

Morning mist settling across the valleys of the Wildlands.

And in turn, it has breathed life back into us.

The silence of those early lockdown months has been replaced by new sounds: the hum of insects, the high call of a kestrel, the rustle of a Tamworth pig moving through long grass. Our White Park cattle graze slowly through the valley, disturbing the soil just enough to make space for wild flowers and the wildlife that follows. Butterflies – like the marbled white and silver-washed fritillary – are now regularly seen, and dragonflies such as the golden-ringed and keeled skimmer have become familiar sightings. Rarer species have emerged too, like the western bee-fly. I think of what it once was: fields regimented for production or sport. And what it is now becoming: a mosaic of habitats, a story still unfolding.

It began with stillness, with a child's brave act, and with a family willing to ask different questions. Today, Mapperton Wildlands stands as a quiet revolution rooted in listening, guided by principle and shaped by hope.

ABOVE Aerial view of the Wildlands showing restored habitat mosaics and regenerating scrub. OVERLEAF Rolling landscape of the Wildlands within the wider West Dorset countryside.

Edward Montagu
1st. Earl of Sandwich

The 1st Earl of Sandwich, from Cromwell's Ally to Restorer of the Monarchy

THERE IS SOMETHING ARRESTING about walking through Mapperton or even Hinchingbrooke House – where we still have a close relationship with the now school – and coming face-to-face with Edward Montagu, the 1st Earl of Sandwich (1625–1672): his portrait hanging calmly on the wall, his gaze fixed somewhere just past the present. I've stood before that portrait countless times and still find myself wondering: how did this man, born into a family of rising gentry, navigate one of the most volatile chapters in English history with both cunning and conviction? And perhaps more provocatively – what would he think of us now?

Edward's story isn't just the stuff of textbooks. It is personal. He is our ancestor. His choices didn't just shape the fate of a country but also laid the very foundation of our family's legacy.

Born in 1625, Edward came of age as England was tearing itself apart. The monarchy was crumbling, Parliament was in open revolt, and society was realigning itself along radical new lines. The Montagus had only recently arrived at the upper reaches of landed society. Edward's father, Sir Sidney Montagu, had purchased Hinchingbrooke House in 1627 – just two years after Edward's birth – and even that detail contains layers of historical tension. The house had been owned by none other than Oliver Cromwell's uncle. That name – Cromwell – would, of course, come to loom large in Edward's life.

From the start, Hinchingbrooke was no ordinary family home. Its history was soaked in politics and symbolism. For Edward, it must have felt like standing at a crossroads from a very early age – a boyhood framed by a house steeped in Royalist loyalty, and yet also tethered, almost fatefully, to the man who would later help to dismantle the monarchy.

Educated at Westminster School and Trinity College, Cambridge, Edward had all the hallmarks of a typical gentry son. But his life would be anything but typical. When civil war broke out, Edward shocked many by siding with the Parliamentarians, even though his father had been a staunch Royalist. I sometimes wonder what that family conversation sounded like. Was it a calculated decision? Youthful rebellion? Or did he, like so many in his generation, believe in reform – at least at first?

By his twenties, Edward had carved out a formidable reputation as a naval commander. He was clever, strategic and, most importantly, adaptable. And this is where I think Edward becomes most fascinating. Because while he rose through the Commonwealth ranks, serving as General at Sea and forging a close association with Cromwell, he never quite severed his connection to the monarchy. His correspondence reveals not a traitor or a zealot, but a pragmatist – someone always watching for the shifting winds.

Portrait of Edward Montagu, 1st Earl of Sandwich, full length in peers robes by Sir Peter Lely.

THE EARL OF SANDWICH
By SIR PETER

By 1660, Edward sensed those winds changing. With Cromwell dead and the Protectorate unravelling, he made his move. And what a move it was. He led the fleet to bring Charles II back from exile: restoring the monarchy and, with it, his own fortunes. That single act redefined him. He became the 1st Earl of Sandwich, Viscount Hinchingbrooke and Baron Montagu of St Neots. His transformation from Cromwellian commander to royal favourite was complete.

The titles themselves are telling. *Hinchingbrooke* rooted him to the family seat; *Sandwich*, the ancient Cinque Port in Kent, nodded to his naval prowess. It was a carefully crafted legacy – a man of land and sea, loyalty and flexibility. Titles, in Edward's case, were more than just honours; they were narrative tools, shaping how history would remember him.

But titles and rewards came with responsibilities – and scrutiny. Edward went on to serve as Ambassador to Portugal and Spain, Master of the Wardrobe, and again took up naval command. Not all of his appointments were successful. There were whispers of mismanagement, misfortune and missteps. And yet he remained dogged in service.

In 1672, at the Battle of Solebay during the Third Anglo-Dutch War, Edward died at sea off the Suffolk coast – his flagship set ablaze by a Dutch fireship. He chose to go down with his men. That choice, to perish with honour, has always struck me. There's something undeniably cinematic about it: tragic, yes, but resolute.

What I keep returning to is how Edward Montagu, 1st Earl of Sandwich, was a man of contradictions: a Parliamentarian who helped to restore a king; a reformer who became a peer; a commander who died not in triumph but in sacrifice. He was not a man of fixed ideology. He was a man of timing, loyalty and ambition woven together in a way that feels modern.

FACING After Sir Peter Lely, portrait of Edward Montagu, 1st Earl of Sandwich, wearing the insignia of the Order of the Garter.
ABOVE (*left*) After Samuel Cooper, portrait of Oliver Cromwell.
(*right*) Portrait of Edward Montagu, 1st Earl of Sandwich, as a young man by Sir Peter Lely.

JOURNAL
FROM SEPT 24 1666 TO MAY 14. 1667 VOL. 3.
THE WEST INDIES
RURAL SPORTS
EARL OF SANDWICH'S JOURNAL
EARL OF SANDWICH'S JOURNAL
FROM AUG. 12. 1669 TO JULY 19: 1671 VOL. 10.
CROOKE'S DESCRIP. OF THE BODY
COLLECT OF TREATIS &C
HISTORIE OF DON QUIXOTE OF THE MANCHA
HISTORIE OF DON QUIXOTE OF THE MANCHA
SCRAP BOOK

The 1st Earl and the Objects of a Tumultuous Century

OF ALL THE STORIES told at Mapperton, few captivate visitors more than those surrounding the 1st Earl. His presence lingers in the house – not just in portraits or family trees, but in three remarkable objects. These pieces bring us close to the man who helped to change the course of English history, and they continue to spark wonder, curiosity and even a few goosebumps on house tours.

We begin in the library, where ten volumes of handwritten journals by the 1st Earl are kept. They are unassuming to look at – faded leather bindings, corners softened with age – but open them and you're instantly transported. Montagu began writing in 1652, initially as a ship's log, but over the years these entries became an expansive record of political shifts, naval operations, diplomatic missions and private reflections. They stop in 1671, a year before his death.

What makes these journals so extraordinary isn't just their historical significance – although that is considerable – but the fact that they give us the unfiltered voice of a man who moved between courts, cabins and causes.

And nowhere is that voice more visible than in the journal entry from 23 May 1660. On that day, aboard the *Naseby*, Edward Montagu commanded the ship entrusted with returning the exiled Charles II to England. The journal recounts the moment in beautiful, matter-of-fact prose: the shore lined with 100,000 onlookers, salutes from forty guns, and the solemnity of a long-awaited return. Edward notes that the King came aboard mid-morning, accompanied by the Dukes of York and Gloucester, the Queen of Bohemia, the Princess Royal and the Prince of Orange. Once Charles was on board, the *Naseby* was renamed the *Royal Charles*. It's a powerful image – the ship changing its name in real time, shedding its republican skin under the feet of a returning monarch.

That very moment is embodied in the second object in this collection: a Dutch colonial hardwood Burgermeister's chair, believed to have been made specifically for Charles II. This is not just a chair. This is THE chair. The King's chair.

The craftsmanship is exquisite: a bowed top rail with human head finials, three foliate-pierced oval splats, and a circular seat supported by six leaf-carved cabriole legs ending in paw feet, joined by scrolling stretchers. You don't need to know any of that to feel its presence, but it's all part of the chair's quiet authority. This is where Charles II sat as he sailed across the sea, returning to the land that had executed his father, accompanied by the man – Edward Montagu – who would deliver him back to power.

Journals of Edward Montagu, 1st Earl of Sandwich, containing illustrated notes on diplomacy, naval affairs, science and court life, 1652–1671.

Visitors are inevitably astonished when they learn this. There's a moment – always – when they look again. 'That chair?' Yes, that chair. Over 350 years ago, a king sat there, steadying himself on the deck of the newly renamed *Royal Charles*, headed for the throne.

And yet, the story of Edward Montagu would not be complete without the third piece: a silver-mounted leather bottle, boldly embossed with the coat of arms of none other than Oliver Cromwell. We believe this to be Cromwell's own drinking flask – the one he carried during the brief and tempestuous period when he was Lord Protector. The other side of the bottle is inscribed in Latin: *Olivarius Dei Gra Reip Angliae Scotia et Hiberniae* (Oliver, by the Grace of God, of the Republic of England, Scotland and Ireland).

ABOVE (*left*) Silver-mounted leather flask embossed with the arms of Oliver Cromwell, believed to have been his personal drinking flask during the Protectorate. (*right*) Dutch Colonial Burgermeister chair with human-head finials, pierced splats and carved cabriole legs. FACING Oliver Cromwell's silver-mounted leather flask displayed in the Dining Room.

This flask, remarkably intact, tells the other half of the 1st Earl's story. Here at Mapperton we keep both – Cromwell's flask and the King's chair – under the same roof, in the same collection. It feels fitting. Edward Montagu was trusted by both sides of a civil war. He navigated the Cromwellian court, earning the confidence of the Lord Protector. And then, just as deftly, he turned towards monarchy, helping to orchestrate Charles II's return. These objects – the flask and the chair – aren't in conflict; they're in dialogue. They speak to a man who knew how to bend without breaking, how to serve without losing his self-possession.

We occasionally place Cromwell's flask on the Dining Room table. Not because we want to provoke, but because it's a conversation starter – and that's exactly what these objects should be. They don't just belong in vitrines. They belong in use, in thought, in discussion. The 1st Earl himself might have appreciated that. He was, after all, a man of words – his journals prove it – and a man of action.

Taken together, these three pieces offer a portrait not just of Edward Montagu, but of an England in flux. A country veering between monarchy and republic, torn by ideology and power, looking for solid ground. Montagu was part of that search. He commanded fleets, met foreign kings, dined with Cromwell and knelt before Charles. He survived where others fell. And he left behind these traces – in ink, in wood, in leather – for us to treasure centuries later.

ABOVE Illustrated page from the journals of Edward Montagu, 1st Earl of Sandwich, showing coastal views and naval sketches.
FACING Library interior showing bookcases and carved overmantel detail.

Boughton House, the Portrait We Share

BOUGHTON IN NORTHAMPTONSHIRE is one of the great Montagu houses since it was purchased by Sir Edward Montagu in 1528. It began as a simple Tudor manor, with a Great Hall at its core, expanding gently over the next 150 years as additional courtyards and wings were added. Then, in a transformative two decades, the North Front rose in grand French style, with new state rooms and vast stables crowned by a mansard roof, earning Boughton its reputation as the English Versailles.

This ambitious transformation was led by Ralph Montagu, later 1st Duke of Montagu, a passionate patron of architects, artists and craftsmen. His dream was to bring French beauty to the English countryside. Yet Ralph's original vision was never fully realized – one wing remains empty, and the facades planned for the South and West Fronts never materialized. His son, John, the 2nd Duke, was more drawn to the formal gardens and avenues, developing a landscape of rare refinement. In hindsight, the result is a house of magnificent contradiction: imposing on the outside yet intimate and irregular within, a patchwork of courtyards, staircases, chimney stacks and sloping rooflines.

From Ralph's inheritance in 1684 until John's death in 1749, Boughton was a stage of almost constant activity. Surviving accounts tell of continual building, frequent visitors and endless entertaining. Then it fell quiet. John's daughter Mary married the Earl of Cardigan, and their daughter in turn married into the Scottish Dukes of Buccleuch. Boughton was no longer the family's focal point, and the house was spared the heavy hand of Victorian redesign or overuse. It slept for over a century, visited only occasionally.

In the early twentieth century, Boughton was once again embraced as a home. Today, it remains alive with beauty and purpose – a private residence, yes, but also a treasure house that continues to open its doors to the public.

What makes Boughton truly special is the harmony of its setting and its collections: paintings, tapestries, silver, carpets, needlework and furniture, all preserved in the very rooms they were acquired for. This is no museum. It is a living home reflecting generations of taste, ambition and cultural aspiration – a place that remains, as it always was, a monument to the power of beauty, history and continuity.

At Mapperton, one painting holds a quiet but commanding presence: a portrait of Edward Montagu, 1st Baron Montagu of Boughton. Draped in rich fur, with a confident gaze and the unmistakable ruff of Jacobean England, he stares out from a heavy gilt frame – calm, composed, certain of his place in the world. And for those who pause, this painting becomes

Boughton House.

a portal not just to another time, but to another house, another story, another expression of Montagu identity. For the same portrait hangs at Boughton House.

And it was here, in the early seventeenth century, that Edward Montagu began to shape a new path for the family rooted in loyalty, principle and political acumen. In the fraught aftermath of the Gunpowder Plot in 1605, while many landowning families in the region found themselves under suspicion, Edward moved swiftly to assert his allegiance to the Crown. He personally sponsored the Observance of 5th November Act, calling for an annual day of thanksgiving for the failure of the plot against James I. In doing so, he not only distanced the Montagus from the plotters, but also positioned himself as a man of conscience and pragmatism – qualities that would be rewarded. In 1621, he was elevated to the peerage as Baron Montagu of Boughton.

This was a turning point not just for Edward, but for the Montagu name. Edward himself was the ancestor of the Dukes of Montagu, while two of his brothers became the forebears of the Earls of Manchester and, most relevant to us, the Earls of Sandwich.

In truth, I find it rather moving that this same likeness resides at both Boughton and Mapperton. These two houses never served the same function in the family's history – Boughton was a political powerhouse, a place of courtly display and architectural ambition; Mapperton, by contrast, was never intended as a great seat of power. And yet, now, in the quiet of Mapperton's panelled hall, that same face keeps watch.

Early seventeenth century, portrait of Edward, 1st Lord Montagu of Boughton.

Summer

SUMMER AT MAPPERTON is full on. There's no other way to describe it. It's the season when everything happens at once – and often all in the same day. The gardens are flourishing, the Coach House is busy, the estate is alive with visitors, and we're filming new episodes every week for our YouTube channel. One day we're cleaning the pool on camera, the next I'm deep in the archives or handling eighteenth-century dresses or military uniforms that once belonged to Montagu ancestors. It's all-consuming and I wouldn't have it any other way.

We host weddings almost every weekend during the summer, interspersed with concerts and even open-air theatre on the croquet lawn. Our Coach House – the converted south stable block – is the centre of it all. During the day, it's our cafe and tea house, where guests pause for lunch beneath umbrellas, shaded from the Dorset sun (when it decides to appear), or take shelter inside when the inevitable summer rain arrives. The interior, with its original beams and soft stone walls, has been beautifully restored and offers a warm, inviting space whatever the weather.

Summer is also when I find myself giving the occasional house tour, guiding guests through the rooms where centuries of history – and family – still live. Portraits of Montagu ancestors hang on the panelled walls, their expressions solemn and dignified. But alongside them, scattered here and there, are photographs of our own lives – of Luke and me on our wedding day and of our four children over the years. It's a reminder that this isn't just a historic house. It's still a home.

And in between, I'm at the heart of my archiving projects: not just letters and papers but textiles – all part of the Montagu story. It's painstaking, absorbing work, and summer gives me the momentum to really dive in. But the truth is, it's never done. There's always another letter to digitize, transcribe, file or organize – another trunk to be opened, another fragment of the past waiting quietly to be rediscovered.

Our children are often part of the mix, stepping in to lend a hand at the wedding bar or in the cafe. Mapperton is very much a family-run estate, and summer brings out the best of that spirit. Whether it's helping the team set up for an event or filming a behind-the-scenes video, we're all pitching in, sleeves rolled up, doing what needs to be done.

The seventeenth-century dovecote, a landmark feature situated beside the house and church.

Visitors wander through the gardens – some are true enthusiasts, here to admire the structure and planting; others are families on holiday, their children darting towards the Lost Village or the Beaver Play Area. The estate is alive and kicking. You can hear laughter, footsteps on gravel, birdsong and sometimes the distant clink of glassware being set out for a wedding.

Of course, there's always a chair to be mended, a leak to stop, Wi-Fi to restore after it goes kaput or a last-minute request to manage, and the list of what still needs doing is as long as ever. But summer here is about embracing it all: the motion, the noise, the layers of history and daily life folding into each other.

There's a kind of joy that comes from the sheer momentum of it all. The gates are open. The estate is buzzing. And every so often, in the middle of the whirlwind, I'll pause for a second – in the archives, in the garden, in the Coach House – and think: 'This is what living history really looks like.'

ABOVE A Renaissance table in the Hall displaying a collection of family photographs. FACING Montagu letters, diaries, journals and photographs preserved in the Muniment Room. OVERLEAF The view west towards the Coach House, crowned with elegant eighteenth-century eagle finials.

COURT
COURT
LETTERS
INDEX

Jacobean Vision

MAPPERTON MAY BE rooted in the Tudor period, but much of what gives the house its visual harmony and day-to-day liveability today comes from the remarkable reimagining of the estate in the seventeenth century. It was during the time of Richard Brodrepp II, beginning around the 1660s, that Mapperton shifted from a charming manorial house to a more structured and impressive estate.

Richard had inherited the estate just after the end of the English Civil War and set about making Mapperton a more fitting reflection of the times. His most visible contribution was the rebuilding of the west-facing Hall wing, which now forms the formal entrance front of the house. With its two-storey elevation, cross-mullioned windows and bold projecting cornice, it presents a confident yet understated face that stands proudly but without pretension.

It must be noted that, technically, the Jacobean period covers work up to the end of the English Civil War; Brodrepp's post-war enhancements are considered Stuart, but the family habitually refers to them as Jacobean.

Inside the house, Brodrepp reshaped the spaces with the same measured clarity he brought to the exterior. One of the most telling architectural details from his time is the arched porch that leads into the Hall – a handsome, semi-enclosed entry with paired niches topped by inverted scallop shells. This motif, echoed in other West Country houses of the period, hints at shared masons and pattern books, but here at Mapperton it feels entirely individual. The porch announces, quietly but deliberately: you are entering somewhere considered.

Step through and the Hall reveals itself – a space that likely evolved under Richard's direction. The oak panelling, traditionally attributed to this period, lends the room its depth and quiet dignity consistent with Jacobean design. In summer, the light from the windows touches the timber floorboards and draws warmth from the panelling, giving the space a soft, enveloping glow. The effect is subtle but theatrical. This is the room that grounds the house: steady, composed and enduringly alive.

And while the Hall holds court, it's the layout beyond that reveals how Brodrepp truly reshaped Mapperton. His defining move – both architecturally and symbolically – was the creation of the two stone stable blocks, one to the north and one to the south. Their placement, flanking both the church and the house, creates an elegant, almost collegiate arrangement that still defines the estate's structure today. It's thought that these stables were built on the site of former village houses whose occupants died during the Great Plague of 1665–6 – a quiet, sobering layer beneath the symmetry. Mapperton, like so many

Richard Brodrepp's Coat of Arms.

country estates, carries traces not only of taste and inheritance, but of loss and survival too.

The south stable block, with its keystone dated 1670, once housed carriages. Today, that building is known as the Coach House – one of the busiest and most versatile spaces on the estate. In 2018, we converted it into a light-filled cafe and event venue, with an industrial kitchen. During the summer, we host everything from wedding celebrations to lectures and concerts. There's something very satisfying about taking a space once built for transportation and filling it with music, light, coffee and cake. It's not repurposing; it's evolution.

The north stable block, by contrast, is still very much doing its time as a glorified storage space. The original horse boxes remain perfectly intact, and just outside is the mounting block, a wonderful little relic of Mapperton's working past. The building's stone is softened by flowering wisteria, which gives it a certain charm in spite of the clutter within. At the moment, it houses everything from garden tools to surplus chairs and crates of event supplies, but one day – one day – I'd love to see it reborn as more accommodation or an exhibition space. The bones are there. It just needs time (and, of course, funding). For now, it waits patiently in the wings, quietly beautiful, and lower on the priority list than it deserves to be.

The Hall interior, revealing layers of architectural detailing and historic fabric.

When Richard Brodrepp began his remodelling in the seventeenth century, he couldn't have known that over 350 years later the buildings he shaped would still be in use – not just admired but animated. There's something incredibly powerful in that continuity. The stables still frame the house. The Hall, with its overmantel and panelling, plays host to wedding guests, volunteers, tourists, a film crew or two and our Christmas tree. And the Coach House? It rarely sees a quiet moment.

Mapperton has never been just a house. It's a conversation – between generations, styles, families and functions. And nowhere is that clearer than in the architectural choices made during its Jacobean reimagining.

In the summer months, that presence is palpable. You feel it in the hum of guests walking from the Coach House to the gardens, in the sound of music warming up for an evening performance, in the sudden stillness of the Hall after a house tour ends. And I feel it, too. Every day I walk these corridors, duck into the archives or watch someone fall in love with the place for the first time.

The arched porch entrance, featuring paired niches with delicately carved inverted scallop shells.

FACING The interior of the north stable block, with original horse boxes dating back approximately 350 years. ABOVE The South Stable Block, now the Coach House Cafe. RIGHT The mounting block at the entrance to Mapperton, once used by riders and carriage passengers.

Pools and Summer House

SUMMER IS WHEN THE gardens at Mapperton really come into their own. The formal terraces hum with bees and colour, each level more vibrant than the last. Lavender and catmint billow along the edges of the upper borders, their scent rising in the heat of the day. Below, salvias, cosmos and rudbeckias fill the beds around the fountain, each bloom competing for attention. The yew hedges and topiary hold it all in place, giving the garden a sculpted calmness even when the planting is at its most exuberant.

This part of the garden was the vision of Ethel Labouchere. Inspired by classical Italianate design, she laid out clipped paths, rills, axial views and symmetry – but always with a softness at the edges. And in summer that balance between formality and flourish reaches its peak.

Just below all of this structure and colour lies one of Mapperton's most unexpected spaces: the natural pools. There are two of them; one is the swimming pool and the other, slightly smaller and covered in lily pads, is what we call the lily pond. The pools have evolved over the centuries, shifting from practical use to something much more beautiful, though still very hands-on to maintain.

Dr Tim Connor, in the *Mapperton* book, suggests that the long rectangular pools below the garden may have been part of a Tudor garden scheme. He notes that the foundations of a two-storey Tudor oriel window once overlooked the valley from above, possibly indicating earlier formal landscaping in this area. While some believe the pools date back to the seventeenth century, others place them in the eighteenth. Either way, they've been here a long time.

In fact, we believe the pools were once used as fisheries, holding a ready supply of live fish for the kitchen. They weren't originally created as a picturesque garden feature, but as something incredibly practical.

Today, the swimming pool is natural – there's no lining, no chlorination and no filtration system humming away in the background. It's fed by a spring higher up the slope. In the early spring, we drain and clean it, usually just before the gardens reopen. It's not a quick process and takes days. We wash down the walls, check for cracks, clear the debris and let the spring water refill it.

What we didn't expect was how *popular* this whole process would become. We filmed the annual cleaning for our YouTube channel, uploaded a few clips to Instagram and TikTok, and then suddenly it was everywhere. The cleaning and draining of Mapperton's pool went viral – millions of views across all platforms. People were absolutely fascinated.

And then, of course, there was me. Swimming in it. This obsession of mine all started during lockdown.

Julie enjoying a swim in Mapperton's spring-fed garden pool.

Like so many of us, I needed something to break up the days – something new, something energizing, something that got me away from my laptop and out of the house. And the pool, freezing as it was, became just that. I'd never tried cold water immersion before, but one chilly morning I decided to give it a go.

The first time, I lasted about thirty seconds – absolutely frozen, gasping, slightly shocked by my own madness. But then I did it again the next day. And the day after that. It became a routine: my thing. Every morning, I'd walk down the steps, climb in (sometimes slowly, sometimes with a squeal), and come out feeling like a new person. It was completely invigorating. I used breathing techniques I'd picked up from yoga to manage the cold, and over time I built up to staying in for two full minutes. I was hooked.

The water never really gets warm. At its coldest, it dips down to 2°C (36°F), and more than once I've had to break through a thin layer of ice just to get in. But there's something about starting the day with that kind of jolt – you're completely present, completely alive.

It's not exactly a solitary swim either. I'm usually sharing the pool with newts, tadpoles and the odd swirl of blanket weed. Dragonflies flit across the surface like they own the place. And there I am – dunking myself under in my now signature swimming cap.

And not just any swimming cap. This one's a proper old-fashioned number, frilly around the edge like something out of a 1950s seaside postcard. I found it years ago tucked away in a drawer somewhere in the house, and now it's part of the Mapperton swimming

FACING (*top left*) Draining, cleaning and repairing the garden pool. (*top right*) Pergola and summer house. (*bottom left*) Interior of the summer house overlooking the pools. (*bottom right*) Fireplace within the summer house. ABOVE Mapperton's natural pools, comprising the swimming pool and the lily pond.

uniform – at least for me. It makes regular appearances in my cold dip videos and, judging by the comments, has developed something of a following all its own.

Because the pool doesn't have a filtration system, we had to get creative. Raymond, our ever-resourceful Clerk of Works (see page 154), and I designed and built twelve floating aquatic plant islands. Each is about a metre square and planted with a mix of lilies, mint and other aquatic plants. They're not rooted in soil, so the roots grow long, trailing down into the water to find nutrients. And that's exactly the point – the roots do the work, drawing out what the algae would otherwise feed on. It's not a flawless system – blanket weed still pops up from time to time – but the floating islands are doing a pretty good job for now.

Just above the pools sits the summer house. It's a small stone building – simple and solid – with one mullioned window and a single door that opens out to the formal gardens. We think it may once have served as a mill or millhouse, given its location just below the spring and above what were likely the estate's historic fisheries. While there are no surviving records to confirm it, the structure feels more practical than decorative.

There's a fireplace inside, which may have been added later – possibly by Ethel Labouchere – since it seems unlikely a working mill or millhouse would have needed one. The rest of the room is bare, but it looks out across the formal gardens and down towards the pools. We believe Mrs Labouchere may have used the summer house to paint from as the light is soft and the setting simple.

We also know that Mrs Labouchere extended her influence into this lower part of the garden. She introduced topiary to either side of the pools, added benches and cranes around a central paved area, and installed a raised octagonal urn. Four cylindrical yews

were planted above the southernmost retaining wall, and piers topped with stone balls helped define the edge of the 1927 formal gardens.

The summer house is not a space we use. It's simply there, quietly keeping watch over the garden Ethel created along with the pools below that once served the house and now – oddly enough – host a rather devoted swimmer in a frilly cap.

FACING The pergola in lush summer growth.
ABOVE The pool with floating aquatic plant islands.
OVERLEAF The lily pond framed by clipped hedging and roses.

Caroline Montagu

11TH COUNTESS OF SANDWICH

When I think of Mapperton, I often think of Caroline, my mother-in-law, who arrived here in the 1980s with my father-in-law, John, and set about the extraordinary task of saving the estate from near collapse.

So much of what we enjoy today was shaped by her determination in those difficult early years. Mapperton in summer now feels open, abundant and alive, but it is easy to forget that it was once bankrupt and neglected. Caroline and John's perseverance gave Mapperton another life. To sit with her and hear those stories was to glimpse not just the history of this house, but the grit and resilience it takes to keep a place like this standing.

JULIE When you and John first arrived to run Mapperton, what were those early days like?

CAROLINE The hardest part about answering any of these questions is deciding how precise I should be. When we finally came down to Dorset in the early 1980s to run the estate, we lived first in the Old Rectory before moving into the big house itself. Running the estate was, frankly, absurd. It was virtually bankrupt. The cottages brought in only about £200 a year in rent. My father-in-law, 'Hinch' as he was known, was getting a bit old and losing his grip, though he didn't realize it; he was also extremely difficult. Everything had to be managed so that he thought it was his idea, or never saw it had happened, especially in the garden, which he loved.

JULIE And you were all living under the same roof?

CAROLINE Yes, for several years once John and I moved into the big house. He had an unvarying routine at mealtimes. He changed into a dark blue velvet smoking jacket for dinner, which he would have in the dining room, just as if it were still the Edwardian age. It was quite common to change for dinner in big houses in the 1980s. Two courses at lunch, three at dinner. I told him I simply couldn't change for dinner every night and – mercifully – he allowed that.

JULIE And meanwhile, you were both commuting to London?

CAROLINE Yes, we were back and forth. Our children were in London schools, so we divided ourselves. I was working as a business and oil journalist writing on Saudi Arabia, while also running Mapperton with the help of an excellent secretary. John was working full time on international development for Christian Aid. One cold March day, in a pub garden near Shaftesbury, we finally decided we couldn't have 'careers' – only jobs. Mapperton came first.

JULIE And yet you turned the estate around. How?

CAROLINE We worked very hard and we sacked quite a lot of people – bank manager, agent, lawyer, accountant – and built our own team. We brought in a marvellous retired surveyor who helped us restore cottages, build and rebuild houses, and even sort out the nightmare of the kitchen. When we moved in the kitchen was only for 'staff'; it had terrible curtains, pipes running along the ceiling and a black asphalt floor covering. We got rid of most of the pipes, changed the curtains to some incredibly expensive French material, and I started picking at the black flooring and discovered the original flagstones underneath. We got rid of all the asphalt, treated the stone and transformed the room.

JULIE Didn't you also uncover things room by room?

CAROLINE Yes, whenever I went into a room, I started pulling at things and looking at fireplaces and materials. The surveyor used to despair of me, but it worked. Over the years, we repaired and reupholstered almost every piece of furniture. The Drawing Room, for example, we turned into a proper country house drawing room with lovely furniture and pictures, somewhere you would want to go after dinner.

JULIE And, meanwhile, your father-in-law kept to his strict routine?

CAROLINE Always. Breakfast at eight, lunch at one, tea in the Orangery at half past four, a vodka and something before his bath at seven, dinner at half past seven, television and bed. At half past two every afternoon, he would go out on his tractor to prune trees and shrubs. It was his routine that kept him going.

JULIE And the gardens?

CAROLINE They were in a dreadful state. We didn't have enough staff, so John, Hinch and I used to clip the yew hedges. I did a lot and increased the variety of shrubs and trees. The gardens only really came into their own about fifteen or twenty years ago. But Hinch had already made his mark – he'd doubled their size, built the Orangery in 1968 and planted the arboretum. He was brilliant at planting trees. Later, John and I added the avenue of chestnuts, inspired by Victorian plans, after the great storm of 1991.

JULIE You also brought in events – the courtyard fair, the plant fair.

CAROLINE Yes. We loved those events; they turned Mapperton from a bit of a gloomy place dominated by my father-in-law into somewhere open, generous and welcoming. That was always what I intended, and we had lots of people to stay.

JULIE You must have some fond memories.

CAROLINE Oh yes, anecdotes. After *Far from the Madding Crowd* finished filming in the courtyard, John and I looked out from the Chapel Room Bedroom window, so relieved the film crew had gone, only to see a whole flock of sheep trotting across the bridge straight into the front courtyard. It was surreal and hilarious. And then there were the great parties – the Asterix Ball with five hundred guests seated in a tented Fountain Court, and the Easter, Christmas and carol services which my father and John revived at All Saints Church. Lovely moments.

JULIE So, after nearly forty years at the helm, what are you most proud of?

CAROLINE Turning it around. Mapperton was nearly bankrupt, in disrepair, and it had a cold, selfish atmosphere. We transformed it into a working estate and, more importantly, a house people wanted to come to – a place that felt warm, open and alive.

FACING The Fountain Court in summer, with formal stonework and manicured planting in full growth. OVERLEAF Lavender and long grasses growing along the bank above the pools.

White Park Cattle

OF ALL THE CREATURES that have come to define the Mapperton Wildlands, none carry such quiet authority as the White Park cattle. They move slowly across the fields and through the woods, their broad horns curving upwards like ancient crowns. With their distinctive white coats, black noses and dark-tipped ears, they seem almost prehistoric – living reminders of a landscape before enclosures and boundaries.

The breed itself is one of the oldest in Britain, dating back at least a thousand years. Herds of White Parks were once kept in the deer parks of medieval monasteries and great houses, managed much like fallow deer. Over centuries, these hardy cattle adapted to survive on poor forage and in challenging weather conditions – characteristics that make them invaluable today in a rewilding landscape. By the twentieth century, however, their numbers had dwindled dramatically. Classified as a rare breed, they were saved by a handful of dedicated people who understood that to lose the White Park would be to lose a piece of Britain's agricultural heritage.

At Mapperton, the decision to bring them into the Wildlands was both practical and symbolic. We needed large herbivores to manage the land – to graze, trample and open up scrub so that light and life could return. And so the White Parks became the very first animals to step into this new project. They were the pioneers, the beginning of a bold experiment to let the land breathe differently. White Parks, with their resilience and their history, were the perfect fit. They are not intensive grazers like modern cattle bred for maximum yield; instead, they browse hedges, graze rough pasture, and create a mosaic of habitats simply through the rhythm of their movement. Where they graze, wild flowers emerge. Where they tread, insects thrive. And in their wake, the landscape becomes more diverse, more alive.

Watching them at Mapperton is always a grounding experience. They are muscular, powerful animals, yet astonishingly calm. For me, however, their size and those formidable horns are a reminder of something else: I am actually rather afraid of cows. It's an irrational fear, and no amount of sensible explanations about temperament or behaviour has ever quite dispelled it. So when the first White Parks arrived at Mapperton, I watched them from behind the gate, keeping a very healthy distance. Over time, though, I have learned to trust them to go their own quiet way. They are nothing like the unpredictable dairy herds I used to avoid in fields; instead, these animals move with deliberate calm, as if they know they carry centuries of history on their backs. Still, I admit that whenever I walk through the Wildlands and see them ahead of me, I find myself plotting the nearest exit route – just in case!

White Park cattle grazing freely within the Wildlands at Mapperton.

This mixture of awe and apprehension is, I think, part of what make the White Parks so special here. They are not tame, not domesticated in the way we expect livestock to be. They retain a sense of the wild, and that is exactly the point. Rewilding at Mapperton is about creating space for natural processes, not about control. The White Parks remind us of that every day: they are here to shape the land, not to be shaped by us.

Bringing them here also revived a connection between country houses and ancient cattle breeds. It was not lost on us that White Parks once roamed the medieval deer parks of families like the Montagus. Now, centuries later, they are back on Montagu land, shaping it once more. There is a certain continuity in that – a reminder that rewilding is not just about the future, but about recovering something of the past.

Of course, keeping White Parks is not without its challenges. Their horns are impressive, and their instinctive caution means they are not always easy to handle. But in the Wildlands, this independence

is a strength. They range freely across hundreds of acres, moving through woodland and pasture in ways that echo the old parkland herds. They require little intervention, thriving as they would have centuries ago, and in doing so they restore something to the land that machinery or modern breeds could never replicate.

They are also ambassadors, drawing visitors into the Mapperton Wildlands story. People are fascinated when they learn about the breed's long history, their near extinction and their crucial role in the future of British biodiversity.

For us, the White Parks embody the spirit of rewilding at Mapperton. They are ancient yet renewed, practical yet symbolic. They remind us that landscapes flourish when shaped by creatures that have always known how to live within them. And every time I see those horns, I am reminded of just how much life and history is carried in their presence – even if I still keep a respectful distance.

FACING Aerial view showing White Park cattle dispersed across the estate landscape. ABOVE A group of White Park cattle within the wider open landscape of the Wildlands.

Louisa, 6th Countess of Sandwich, Letters, Love and Legacy

I USED TO THINK OF Louisa Montagu (1781–1862) purely in terms of Hinchingbrooke – the Dowager Countess, the woman who held the household together by advising her son, the 7th Earl of Sandwich, after her husband died in 1818 and the fire swept through the south wing of Hinchingbrooke House in 1830. But the letters in the Muniment Room tell a richer story. They show a woman who lived at the intersection of public duty and private influence – not just at Hinchingbrooke, but in the social worlds of London, Paris and even, remarkably, Napoleon's Elba.

Born Lady Louisa Lowry-Corry, the daughter of Armar Lowry-Corry, 1st Earl Belmore, and Lady Harriet Hobart, she grew up between London and her family's great seat in Ireland, Castle Coole. In 1804 she became engaged to George John Montagu, Viscount Hinchingbrooke, heir to the Earl of Sandwich. Among the correspondence we hold at Mapperton House are letters filled with warmth, delight and a clear sense of expectation for her future. They reveal that to her family and closest friends she was simply 'Lou', and they show the intimacy of her circle – from her vivacious half-aunt Lady Castlereagh, who wasted no time in sharing the news, to distant cousins and great political hostesses who felt compelled to write at once. The 6th Marchioness of Queensberry, Caroline Douglas, exclaimed, 'And so Lou is going to be married . . . I have made up my mind to seeing you and hearing from you less (two of the things in the world I like best) if Ld. H [Lord Hinchingbrooke] will promise to make you very very happy and to love you better than ever husband loved a wife before.'

From Scotland, her cousin Henry Montagu sent his own warm assurance: 'Seriously my dearest Lou you cannot think of how happy it has made me to hear you were going to be secured to us on this Side of the Water and married to a person we have all known and liked all of our lives.'

Through their words, we see Lou as both beloved niece and admired young woman – a figure whose marriage was celebrated not just within her family, but across a network of aristocratic households from London drawing rooms to Scottish ducal estates.

Marriage brought Lou into the heart of political and court life. George served in senior positions under Lord Liverpool – one of Britain's longest-serving prime ministers – and her life became a rhythm of London seasons, court receptions and visits to the Continent.

It was on one such journey, in 1814, that she found herself face to face with history. Napoleon Bonaparte, newly exiled to the island of Elba after his abdication, had become an object of fascination for Europe. In Lou's own words:

Portrait of Louisa, 6th Countess of Sandwich (1781–1862), whose letters, diaries and artistic works survive in the Mapperton archive.

LADY SANDWICH
1840.

> The day after our arrival we were walking near the Emperor's country house when he passed us in his carriage & sent back one of his escort to desire us to come on to his house . . . for four hours he talked almost incessantly of Emperors, Kings, Ministers, Battles, Intrigues . . . of which he gave the most amusing account . . . This is something in one's life to have passed four hours in active conversation with such a man, to have laughed with him, disputed with him . . . in fact to have seen with the sort of ease that one does any private gentleman, a man who has governed so many nations, made & unmade so many kings & who since Alexander or Ceasar is certainly the most extraordinary character of whom history can speak.

For Lou, Europe was never just a backdrop but part of her lived experience. If Elba offered her a glimpse of an emperor in exile, then Paris provided her with a stage of a different sort: one of refinement, sociability and taste. Not only did she take an apartment there, but she moved within a world where the British aristocracy was beginning to mingle once more with Continental elites in the fragile peace after Waterloo. Several beautiful pieces of furniture in the family collection today came from her time in the city. They're objects I'll return to in the pages that follow, and they hint not only at Lou's eye for quality but at her connections in this wider post-Napoleonic society – a world that helps make sense of her later approval when her daughter Caroline married Count Walewski, Napoleon's son.

When George died in 1818, Louisa became Dowager Countess. Her attention turned to her children and the preservation of the family's standing. In the years that followed she settled into the role of matriarch, guiding her son John as he stepped into the title of 7th Earl, and arranging good marriages for her daughters. Her correspondence from this period reveals a woman attentive to both duty and affection, combining practical advice with the gentle firmness of one who expected to be heard.

It was against this backdrop of steady family stewardship that disaster struck. In 1830, there was a devastating fire at Hinchingbrooke: 'A fire broke out in the south wing and in spite of all exertions it burnt with such fury that nothing could be saved from that part of the house. The rooms are entirely destroyed and the walls much injured. It is a grievous sight, but I trust we shall rebuild it better than before.'

The rebuilding fell formally to her son, but Lou's voice is present in the correspondence – practical, determined and unshaken. The restored Hinchingbrooke blended what could be salvaged with new designs fit for the nineteenth century, ensuring the house remained both a family seat and a place capable of hosting political and social life.

She was remembered as serious, devout and principled – but the Lou of her letters is also worldly, observant and quietly strategic. Today, her portrait hangs at Mapperton House, her gaze steady and composed. And now, thanks to her own words, we can see that steadiness for what it truly was: the product of a life lived at the centre of history, and a woman who understood that legacy is as much about adaptation as it is about tradition.

FACING (*top*) One of Louisa's original paper portfolios, still containing correspondence from her years as Countess of Sandwich.
(*bottom*) A portfolio label reading 'Lady Sandwich 1840', preserved with Louisa's drawings.

A collection of Louisa's sketchbooks and correspondence.

MARY of MODENA

Louisa's Hand

EVERY SO OFTEN, Mapperton reveals something that takes my breath away. Sometimes it's a small, unexpected discovery – a forgotten sketchbook in the back of a drawer. Other times it's a long-lost treasure that suddenly reappears in the most unlikely of ways, ready to come home.

This chapter is about some of those moments. First, the thrill of finding Louisa's hand-painted miniatures – tiny but powerful portraits of great women of history – which had been lost for decades before making their way back here. Then there's her own suite of Regency rosewood furniture, now in the Drawing Room, where one day I pulled open a drawer and found her sketchbook, signed Louisa Corry and dated 1803, the year before her marriage to George. And finally, the letters and diaries that open up her world: the invitations, the travel journals and her extraordinary correspondence in French with her son-in-law Count Walewski, Napoleon's illegitimate son.

THE MINIATURES

One of the most thrilling acquisitions in recent years has been the return of four miniature portraits painted by Louisa. These exquisite works – two from her years as Viscountess and two as Countess – had vanished from the collection decades ago until, rather wonderfully, one of our YouTube viewers contacted me to say they had spotted them for sale on eBay.

The seller turned out to be based just a few miles from Mapperton. I quickly got in touch, launched an online fundraiser, and thanks to the generosity of our supporters, we were able to bring them home. From an old Christie's receipt, we know there were originally six miniatures in the set, which was sold in 1956. Four have resurfaced; two are still missing. I hold on to the hope that one day they too will reappear. For now, these four are treasured reminders of Louisa's remarkable skill. Far from amateur experiments, they are delicate and accomplished likenesses, testifying to her artistic talent.

THE FURNITURE AND SKETCHBOOK

Louisa's years as Dowager Countess also left their mark on the collection we see today. After George's death, she spent long periods of time in Paris, where she took an apartment. Several pieces of French furniture from these years in Paris survive at Mapperton – rosewood with marquetry and gilt details that reflect her taste and her time on the Continent. In the Drawing Room is her suite of Regency rosewood furniture, richly

FACING Miniature portraits painted by Louisa arranged beside her sketchbook and watercolours. OVERLEAF The Drawing Room at Mapperton, home to several pieces of French and Regency furniture associated with Louisa's years on the continent.

decorated with brass and boxwood stringing, with flourishes such as sphinx-headed capitals and rope-twist legs. Fashionable in its day, it remains one of the highlights of a visit.

It was while carefully inspecting one of these pieces – the Carlton House writing table – that I made perhaps my most exciting personal discovery. Opening a drawer, I came across Louisa's own sketchbook, containing a series of pencil and wash drawings. Two of the earliest are carefully inscribed 'copied from Guercino' and dated 1803. Giovanni Francesco Barbieri, known as Guercino (1591–1666), was one of the great painters of the Italian Baroque, celebrated for the movement and emotion in his figures. For young women of Louisa's class, copying Old Masters was considered an essential part of artistic education, a way to train the eye and the hand. That she chose Guercino – and executed her copies with such assurance – speaks volumes about her taste and ambition. The skill is remarkable: the drapery, the expressions, the delicate use of wash. These are not the hesitant exercises of a beginner, but confident studies by a young woman with genuine talent.

A year later, in 1804, is a finely executed profile of George himself. To hold in my hands a sketch Louisa made of her future husband, preserved within her own sketchbook and discovered tucked away inside her writing table, was nothing short of extraordinary. Had it lain there since she last opened it more than two centuries ago? I cannot know, but I like to imagine so.

ABOVE (*top*) A pencil profile of George Montagu, sketched by Louisa in 1804. (*bottom*) One of the sphinx-headed capitals decorating Louisa's Regency rosewood writing furniture. FACING Part of Louisa's Regency rosewood library furniture, richly decorated with brass inlay and sphinx-headed mounts.

Le Comte BATTHYANY
Chambellan
et Lieutenant-Colonel au service
de S. M. l'Empereur d'Autriche.
Le Comte et la Comtesse de Bützow
IL MARCHESE DI FUSCALDO avendo ottenuto dalla Maestà del RE suo Padrone il permesso di solennizzare il giorno Onomastico di S. M. il RE CARLO IV. prega la Sig.ra Contessa de Sandwich di voler passare la serata del giorno 4. Novembre 1818. in questo Real Palazzo Farnese, per far corte ai prefati Augusti Sovrani ad un'ora di notte.
Si ballerà alle ore tre di notte.
Marchesa
CLEMENTINA INCONTRI
nata di Briè
PAPA PIO VII
Lady Sandwich
Bachelors at Home
PALAZZO SINIBALDI
Wednesday 3rd Feb.y 1830
Le Marquis de Caraman, ambassadeur de France près la Cour d'Autriche
Milord et Milady Shrewsbury
Les masques ne sont pas admis.
Le Prince Gagarin prie Madame la Comtesse de Sandwich et Lady Caroline Montague de lui faire l'honneur de venir diner à 6 heures chez lui le lundi 28 Decembre
Non potendo intervenire si prega di rimandare

THE LETTERS AND DIARIES

Louisa's world also comes alive through her papers: her travel diaries, her invitations from royalty and, most remarkably, her correspondence with Count Alexandre Walewski, her son-in-law. All of his letters were written in French, and Louisa, of course, was fluent, so their entire exchange unfolded in that language. What is extraordinary is that Walewski's original letters are preserved in the Muniment Room at Mapperton, carefully translated and typed in English by Alberta, ensuring that Louisa's voice and Walewski's words are accessible today.

The Walewski letters are particularly striking, not only for their historical detail but for their intimacy. After his first visit to Hinchingbrooke, Walewski wrote with excitement: 'I will tell you that I am in a transport of joy about Hinchingbrook, it is really a precious building for a family.'

But tragedy shadowed their relationship. In April 1834, Louisa's daughter Caroline – Walewski's wife since 1831 – died in Paris. Less than three months later, he wrote to her brother John, the 7th Earl of Sandwich, in a letter filled with grief:

> I beg you, my dear Sandwich, to always consider me as a brother, if I live a thousand years, I shall never forget the touching scene I witnessed on your arrival in Paris, when you saw your poor sister again, she was so glad to kiss you and when I told her you had arrived she cried, 'Oh dear, dear, Sandwich, let him come in directly.' I cannot think of those remarks without emotion. You have certainly lost much, but not as much as I have, we had completely become one, and now, I feel lost and lonely.

The following year, sorrow deepened when Louisa's grandson – Caroline and Walewski's little boy – also died. Walewski's letter to Louisa is heartbreaking:

> My dear Lady Sandwich, one hour before my departure, my poor little boy's short life ended . . . what grieved me most in this event was that it brought back the memory of the irreparable misfortune which I experienced last year, upsetting my existence and which I shall never forget.

That Walewski continued to write to Louisa, even after such devastating losses and even after he himself remarried, speaks volumes about the depth of their relationship. These letters, when read alongside Louisa's diaries – full of sharp observations on her travels and society in Paris – paint a portrait of a woman deeply engaged in the world, fluent in languages, skilled with pen and brush, and connected to some of the most fascinating figures of her age.

FACING A selection of invitations, visiting cards and social ephemera from Louisa's papers, reflecting the wide social world recorded in her correspondence and diaries. OVERLEAF *(left page)* A marble bust of Louisa, 6th Countess of Sandwich, displayed above one of the Regency writing tables associated with her suite of furniture at Mapperton. *(right page)* A study from Louisa's sketchbook, copied after Guercino in 1803.

Castle Coole, Louisa's Childhood Home

IF MAPPERTON HAS ITS honey-gold Ham stone and Hinchingbrooke its Huntingdonshire red brick, then Castle Coole in Fermanagh, Northern Ireland is all pale Portland stone grandeur – James Wyatt's most celebrated neoclassical masterpiece. Wyatt, one of the most fashionable architects of the late eighteenth century, was renowned for his elegant classical designs and for reshaping the architectural landscape of Georgian Britain. Rising out of its wooded parkland, Castle Coole was conceived not simply as a home but as a statement.

The Lowry-Corry family had already been substantial landowners in Ireland for generations, their estates built up through judicious marriages and alliances. When Armar Lowry-Corry, Louisa's father, inherited Castle Coole in 1779, he was ambitious to secure both political influence and social standing. His solution was architecture. By commissioning Wyatt to design an imposing new house, he intended Castle Coole to serve as both a family seat and a declaration of power and permanence.

Castle Coole was built on a heroic scale for Ireland. Wyatt, at the height of his career, never visited the site, instead sending his designs from London. Portland stone was shipped at enormous expense, while local builders and joiners executed the architect's designs. The plaster ceilings remain some of the finest examples of neoclassical decoration in Ireland. The house was completed in 1797, just as the earlier Georgian house on the site burned down, leaving this new creation to stand in splendid isolation.

The interiors were fitted out in the grand Regency style, with the most remarkable commission, the State Bed, created in expectation of a visit by the Prince Regent, later George IV. He never came, but the bed – towering, gilded and little used – survives in near-pristine condition, one of the best preserved of its kind.

Castle Coole's fortunes mirrored those of many great houses. Built at enormous cost, it left Louisa's father deeply in debt. Though it passed securely through the family in the nineteenth century, the twentieth brought the challenges that threatened so many estates: taxation, the decline of land-based wealth and the sheer expense of maintenance. By 1951, Castle Coole had been sold to the government and transferred to the National Trust.

The twentieth century was the great age of destruction for the country house. Never before had so many disappeared in such a short time. It is estimated that around 4,000 of the UK's country houses were demolished or lost between 1875 and 1975, with more than 1,200 of those in England alone after 1900. By the mid-1950s the pace was relentless. SAVE Britain's Heritage later calculated that seventy-five houses

Castle Coole, Louisa's childhood home.

were lost in a single year – about one every five days. Others, such as the architectural historian John Martin Robinson, have put the figure even higher, suggesting that as many as a thousand were destroyed between 1945 and 1955. Many were demolished, others gutted of their contents or converted into hospitals, schools – like Hinchingbrooke – and institutions. Survival could never be taken for granted.

In Louisa's case, both her childhood and married homes were sold, one to the National Trust and the other to the local council. Yet both endured. Today, students still walk through the corridors of Hinchingbrooke, while Castle Coole's columned portico remains one of the great entrances of Georgian Ireland. The irony is that Castle Coole's gleaming facades were faced with Portland stone, quarried just a short distance from Mapperton.

That link between Dorset, Huntingdonshire and Ireland is more than just architectural; it is part of Louisa's story. She grew up among the neoclassical grandeur of Wyatt's interiors at Castle Coole, then crossed to England to marry into the Montagu family at Hinchingbrooke. And while neither house remained in family hands, both endured the upheavals of the twentieth century. In a time that saw so many country houses lost forever, Louisa's homes were spared the wrecking ball – altered, repurposed, but still standing.

Interior at Castle Coole.

Autumn

Autumn at Mapperton is always a turning point. By the time the last visitors leave at the end of the season, we are all absolutely exhausted after months of opening. The chatter in the cafe dies down, the guided tours stop and the house falls into a quieter rhythm. But for Luke and me, it isn't a season of rest. Mapperton doesn't suddenly go still just because the public season has ended.

This is when the house changes character. Instead of visitors passing through, we host a small group of paying guests for our Grand Historic Tour. For nearly a week, they don't just look at the rooms – they live in them. Luke and I are with them during this time, entertaining, sharing stories and opening up the house in a way that feels entirely different from the summer months. It's a concept we created to show Mapperton behind the scenes, and it has become one of the most exciting things we do here.

Outside, autumn transforms the valley. The gardens soften, their lines clearer against the fading colours, while in the arboretum the trees blaze week by week with gold, red and copper. Beyond the terraces, the Wildlands are alive with activity: pigs turning the soil, ponies grazing and browsing, all of them working the land in preparation for spring. Autumn may look like an ending, but here it is full of life.

Inside, with the rooms still and the days shorter, I have more time to spend with the family collection and archives. Autumn gives me a chance to look back as well as forwards, to spend time with the stories of ancestors whose portraits hang on the walls and whose letters and objects lie in drawers and cupboards.

Even as the public season comes to an end and we begin closing the gates, the estate still has moments of real energy. In recent years, our Halloween trail has become one of them. When my children were much younger and we were living in London, I had to rely on my American friends to tell me which mansion blocks to go to for trick-or-treating – it simply wasn't part of the culture in the same way, and I was determined they wouldn't miss out. To now see families arriving at Mapperton, dressed up and enjoying that same sense of excitement, feels like something has come full circle.

Autumn here is a season not of rest but of change. The public may be gone, but the work continues. Mapperton shifts gear, the energy takes a different shape, and the house and estate remain very much alive.

FACING Paperbark maple (*Acer griseum*) displaying its distinctive peeling cinnamon-coloured bark in autumn. OVERLEAF Wellington boots arranged at Mapperton's back-of-house entrance.

The Georgian Face

THE GEORGIAN CONTRIBUTIONS are often overshadowed by Mapperton's showier elements – the flamboyant plaster ceiling of the Tudor Great Chamber or the decorated ceiling of the Drawing Room. Yet step back and you cannot miss the Georgian presence. It was the work of another Richard Brodrepp – not the seventeenth-century owner who gave the house its Jacobean refinements (see pages 89–91), but his descendant a century later, Richard Brodrepp IV, who lived here from 1739 to 1774.

This Richard remade Mapperton for his time. He classicized the North Front, replacing the irregular Tudor mullions with orderly sash windows. And behind that new face he created the Staircase Hall – and it is this space, more than anywhere else, that carries Mapperton into the eighteenth century. The staircase itself is elegant, with a handrail that swells over the newel post in a gesture of quiet confidence. It is unmistakably the work of the Bastard Brothers of Blandford, those master builders who left their mark across Dorset (see page 13). Their joinery has a measured assurance: the balusters are finely turned, the rail is smooth and continuous, the whole flight seems to draw you upwards with ease. Even now, when I climb those stairs, I am reminded that they belong to a broader story of Dorset craftsmanship.

Above that staircase, Richard added a rococo plaster ceiling. It is lighter and more playful than anything the Tudors left behind – curves and flourishes that ripple across the surface. In creating it, Mapperton was making a declaration: it could keep pace with the fashions of the new age.

Richard didn't stop there. In the Library, he introduced another rococo ceiling, even more exuberant. The plasterwork here is all scrolls and swirls with a cherub face showing off in the centre. Stand beneath it and you sense the ambition of the age – a desire for refinement, but also for beauty and display. It is a very different kind of showmanship than the great Tudor ceilings, but no less intentional.

What is striking is that Richard did not seek to transform the entire house. Instead, he left Mapperton with a new face and a pair of interiors that spoke clearly of the eighteenth century, layered on to what was already there. Even from the outside the contrast is obvious. Walk around the house and the story of its history unfolds in stone: to the north, the clean Georgian front with its sash windows, dignified and symmetrical, but to the south and west, you are met with the Tudor and Jacobean outlines that remain intact. Each side belongs to a different century, yet they all meet at the same corners, held together by the whole. Mapperton quite literally wears its history on different faces.

FACING Sash windows set into the elegant Georgian facade of the house. OVERLEAF The north-facing Georgian elevation of the house in autumn light.

With the gentler pace of autumn, I notice the Georgian layers most of all. The Staircase Hall glows in the late afternoon light, the rococo plaster seems to shimmer a little brighter, and the sash windows bring an order to the house's rambling outline. Mapperton, in these months, feels balanced: its Georgian dignity standing alongside the Tudor and Jacobean bones, a reminder that every generation has added its own chapter to this house.

The Georgian staircase, attributed to the celebrated Bastard Brothers of Blandford.

ABOVE The Rococo plaster ceiling of the library. FACING A close detail of a cherub's head from the Rococo plaster ceiling in the library.

Victor's Vision

JUST BEYOND THE clipped discipline of the Fountain Court, the garden begins to loosen its shoulders. This shift was the work of Victor 'Hinch' Montagu, my husband's grandfather. A politician by career but a gardener at heart, Victor left his mark on Mapperton by expanding Ethel's gardens in bold and imaginative ways. By the time he arrived in 1955, the gardens had lost much of their earlier precision. Like so many country estates, Mapperton had endured the upheaval of the Second World War, when staff and resources were stretched thin and maintenance inevitably declined. Mrs Labouchere herself had been unwell for some years before her death, and without her personal involvement the planting grew tangled and overgrown. What Victor inherited was a garden in need of care and vision, and he embraced the task with energy. His work over the following decades not only restored what had been neglected, but also reimagined Mapperton's landscape, extending it with bold new plantings and giving it the character we recognize today.

One of his first challenges came soon after he arrived. In the late 1950s, the majority of the elms and limes to the main drive were felled, leaving only three of the limes in place. The great transformation came with Victor's decision to replant the drive as an avenue of American limes (*Tilia americana*). This choice was no accident. His mother, Alberta, had been American, and Victor was a frequent visitor to his relations across the Atlantic. He admired American gardens, and their influence is clear in the remarkable number of American species he introduced across Mapperton.

The 1960s also brought other changes. The upper pool was lined, transforming it into a swimming pool for the family, a space that remains part of Mapperton's summer life to this day (see pages 95–101). Further down the valley, Victor turned his attention to what became the Arboretum. Victor had the whole area cleared, apart from a scattering of native trees left on the western slope. Into this open space he planted a collection of specimen trees and shrubs, setting them in rough grasses so that they would grow with a freer, more natural character.

His planting notebooks, still carefully kept here, record his choices in neat handwriting – an archive in ink that has since become a living archive of trunks, branches and seasonal displays. Among them were the tulip tree (*Liriodendron tulipfera*), its broad leaves glowing yellow each autumn, and the handkerchief tree (*Davidia involucrata*), famous for its fluttering white bracts in spring and fiery foliage in autumn. That tree was uprooted in a storm not long ago, but Luke has already planted a small replacement. I like to think that seventy years from now someone else will be writing about its beauty just as I am now.

An avenue of American limes lining the drive at Mapperton.

Victor also introduced more unusual specimens, including the metasequoias, or dawn redwoods (*Metasequoia glyptostroboides*), thought to be extinct until rediscovered in China in the 1940s. Each autumn their feathery needles turn a burnished copper before falling in rust-coloured drifts across the grass. At the bottom of the Arboretum, he planted a towering eucalyptus, still thriving today and adding its distinctive fragrance and grey-green leaves to the mix. There are many others too: maples and liquidambars for their blazing reds, chestnuts and oaks for their rich browns, and wonderful magnolias that carry the Arboretum through other seasons. Each was chosen with care, each adding to the Arboretum's variety.

And Victor's planting stretched beyond the Arboretum itself. On the east-facing lawn beside the house, looking out across the gardens, stands a magnificent paperbark maple (*Acer griseum*) planted in the 1960s. Its cinnamon-coloured bark peels in strips, a feature as striking as its leaves. Today the tree is recognized as a Dorset County Champion for its girth, and as it continues to grow, it may yet go on to become a national champion.

My mother-in-law has always said she tries to remain loyal to Victor's planting schemes, guided by his notebook, and I feel the same. To walk here is to step inside his vision. In autumn, especially, the Arboretum changes my sense of the season in a way the formal

ABOVE The garden grotto enveloped in autumn foliage.
FACING *(top)* Victor Montagu's planting notebooks record in neat handwriting the trees, shrubs and planting schemes that continue to shape the garden today. *(bottom left)* Autumn colour along one of Mapperton's winding garden walks. *(bottom right)* Grapes ripening on the pergola in autumn.

Paperbark maple (*Acer griseum*), planted in the 1960s, overlooking the formal gardens in autumn.

gardens never do. The terraces remain composed, their clipped lines hardly altered by the turning year, but here the season shouts its presence. The colours shift week by week. Leaves crunch underfoot, twigs snap and the rustle of the canopy overhead follows you as you walk. The light drops lower and filters through branches in golden shafts. These trees – some now towering giants – remind us that time is passing, and with it the cycle of life at Mapperton keeps turning.

This is the part of the garden I most often walk in, especially in the quieter months. I find myself looking up into the branches of trees Victor planted over half a century ago. The Arboretum isn't just a collection of trees. In autumn it becomes Mapperton at its most alive – bright, fleeting and impossible to ignore.

LEFT The bank above the summer house, softened by autumn planting. ABOVE The peeling cinnamon bark of the paperbark maple (*Acer griseum*).

Raymond Leaf

CLERK OF WORKS

For more than four decades, Raymond Leaf – our head of maintenance, our Clerk of Works – has quietly kept Mapperton running.

Often when I think of Mapperton, I don't just see the house, gardens or archives – I think of Raymond. His work rarely shows up in the photographs, but it's there in everything: a window that opens, water flowing to the cottages, the heat in the boiler, the estate set right after a storm. Over his long tenure, he has quietly held this place together. Mapperton has endured because of people like Raymond, and for that our family – and this house – owe him so much.

JULIE Raymond, thank you for sitting down with me. We pass each other daily, though it's usually about leaks and repairs, so it's so nice to have a proper chat. Let's start at the beginning – when did you first come to Mapperton, and what were you doing at the time?

RAYMOND I came to Mapperton in 1982. A tenant farmer recommended me; Lady Sandwich said there was plenty to do. Back then the family were in and out at weekends – Lord and Lady Sandwich, and Victor Montagu. I was self-employed, so I split my time, but I kept choosing Mapperton. I've been dipping in and out ever since.

JULIE In those early years, what was your work mainly?

RAYMOND Maintenance across the estate – repairs in the tenanted cottages and the farms, and jobs in the main house. Over time I've painted nearly the entire interior of the manor.

JULIE You tackled some big rooms!

RAYMOND The Hall first. Lady Sandwich tried a stronger green on the border; after a couple of weeks we changed course and I went back up. The hardest bit was scrubbing the rococo mouldings clean – ten days on a scaffold. Then the Drawing Room ceiling – hadn't been done since Mrs Labouchere's time, I'd say. We cocooned the pictures in polythene. I also worked on the Library's rococo ceiling and the Hall walls with Nicky Haslam; he was brilliant at tinting. We repainted the Hall overmantel together, bringing back the greens where the paint had worn.

JULIE And the Hall ceiling?

RAYMOND Cleaned twice, carefully. Smoke dulls a surface, and we once had a leak into the ceiling. We had to analyse the layers and found it was an old distemper – that's a chalk-based paint which goes powdery and flakes, so we had to scrub every bit of it off before repainting with the right materials.

JULIE Mapperton as a film location has helped with funding some repairs too.

RAYMOND Then luckily we had *The History of Tom Jones*, and I got involved with decorating the house, taking it right back to Squire Western's colour. We painted all the panelling, and I actually got a friend to help me. We had to scumble stain all of it – that's a painting technique where you drag colour over a base to imitate wood grain, so the panels looked like a richer oak. If you go upstairs, in places behind the radiators, you can still see the dark brown underneath. We put on the scumble stain, then added the markings of grain and carried it all the way down the stairs. Location fees helped: a barn on the estate was thatched, two cottages done, roof works – those jobs got pushed forwards because filming paid for them.

JULIE We also had the devastating storage fire where so much of the paintings and chattels were stored during filming

RAYMOND Dreadful. We'd just had two lorry loads of furniture returned, luckily, or the loss would have been far worse. Even so, we lost pictures and beloved pieces. It was a blow, but Mapperton always seems to bounce back.

JULIE You've seen three clear eras: Victor, then John and Caroline, and now Luke and me. What stands out?

RAYMOND With Victor, a quieter house – routines, records, steady care. With John and Caroline, a long phase of doing up houses as needed – family life in the corridors With you and Luke, a bigger public life – visitors, weddings, coaches, digital reach that brings people here. The house and valley don't change; how you run them does.

JULIE Water, or should I say leaks, is the bane of our lives. We're not on mains, and you're the first call at midnight.

RAYMOND Mapperton's not on mains water – we rely on private reservoirs, which are like large storage tanks, and they feed water across the estate through a network of pipes. We've renewed a lot of pipework and added isolation valves so we can 'sectionalize' and therefore keep tenants and the cafe supplied.

I work closely with our water engineer; day or night, we usually stabilize things quickly.

JULIE Windows and joinery are constant, too.

RAYMOND Always. Mullions move – that's the vertical stone dividing a window – catches loosen so they don't hold properly, and the sash frames swell or get painted over so they stick.

When we scaffold – say on the garden-facing bedrooms – we do as much as possible while it's up. Critical windows first: Dining Room windows by the hot plates, Hall windows by the clock, Library embrasures – anything house tour guide volunteers need to open and close reliably.

JULIE Raymond, we've talked about the repairs, the water and all the daily work that goes into keeping Mapperton running. But looking back over your many years here, what memories stand out most – the ones that have really stayed with you?

RAYMOND Finishing a hard job, looking up and thinking, 'We did that.' Making good after leaks or storms. Watching the family grow – Luke in his youth racing about, then the next generation. And then there was the Asterix party; Lady Sandwich came out one day with some Asterix comics and said, 'We're going to base a party on this.' We didn't even know who Asterix was at the time!

She asked for a palisade across the front courtyard, so we begged and borrowed fencing from local farmers and contractors, put up a great spiked barrier and a grand entrance gate. We boarded over the Fountain Court so people could dance, built platforms for dining on different levels in the garden, and carpets went down everywhere. By the end of the week statues and props had arrived – huge statues made of polystyrene – and the whole place was transformed.

On the day, it felt like Mapperton had become another world. From the steps down to the gardens there was a canopy walkway; there must have been five hundred people in costume, Romans and Gauls, druids and goddesses. A band came from London – the music was unbelievable, echoing off the grottoes – and the party went on and on. I remember leaving at four in the morning, and it was still going. Someone told me Lord Sandwich leaned out of his window around nine o'clock saying, 'Can we stop now?' It was that loud.

There was food everywhere, drinks flowing, even a pig on a spit. It was the day Mapperton let its hair down. People still talk about it locally as one of the most memorable parties ever held here.

JULIE After forty-plus years, why keep coming back?

RAYMOND I love it. I do the rounds daily – the tours, the biomass, the checks. If a pipe bursts, we sort it. If a window sticks, we free it. Mapperton's a living place. You and Luke do it your way; that's how it should be. My job is to keep the wheels turning.

JULIE A final word?

RAYMOND Keep going. Balance the books with films, fairs, weddings – use the income to care for the fabric. Mapperton's always bounced back. Look after it, and it looks after you.

The carved overmantel in the Hall, dated 1604 and originally from Melplash Court, later installed at Mapperton as part of the house's evolving interior history.

Pigs and Ponies Arrive

IF I'M EVER HAVING ONE of those days, I head straight out to find the pigs. They always come running as soon as they see me, their ears twitching and snouts pushing forwards, certain I must have arrived for the sole purpose of giving them a good scratch. The moment I rub behind their ears, they flop over on to their sides, rolling their enormous bodies on the ground and waiting for me to scratch their bellies. Within minutes they are stretched out, half-asleep, snoring softly, perfectly content. They are, without doubt, the happiest and loveliest animals on the estate, and it is impossible not to feel lighter in their company.

Autumn at the Wildlands – as the land begins to shift towards winter – is also when the animals become most visible in the landscape. The Tamworth pigs are busy rootling through wet ground, while the Exmoor ponies graze steadily across the hillsides. Between them, they do the hard work of managing the land: breaking up pasture, creating space for new growth and keeping vegetation in balance.

THE TAMWORTH PIGS

There are just two Tamworths here, but they have the power of a whole herd. Known as 'nature's plough', they spend their days rootling with their snouts, turning over turf and soil in search of roots. After heavy rain, they are relentless – churning through pasture, pulling up stubborn grasses and dock plants, exposing raw earth. At first sight, the ground they leave behind looks messy, almost destructive. But this is exactly their role. By disturbing the soil, they create pockets where new vegetation can grow and they open up habitats for invertebrates.

In autumn this work takes on another layer of meaning. As they root and dig, they create hollows in which they themselves can bed down, finding warmth and shelter when the weather turns wet and cold. Their rootling is both survival and stewardship – providing them comfort while also setting the stage for a richer variety of wild flowers and insects next spring.

THE EXMOOR PONIES

The ponies, by contrast, are more reserved. Exmoors are one of Britain's most ancient breeds, unchanged for thousands of years, with stocky bodies, thick coats and a wild curiosity. They are perfectly suited to life outdoors all year round, even as the winds whip across the hills in November.

Their grazing style complements the cattle: where the White Parks eat higher, the ponies crop close, taking grass right down to the roots. They are selective, too, working

A ladybird rests among the long grasses in the Wildlands, where rewilding has transformed former pasture into habitat for insects and pollinators.

their way through thistles and gorse, nibbling at plants other grazers leave behind. They browse as well as graze, keeping woody scrub in check. And with their hooves they puddle the wet ground, creating small depressions that fill with water after autumn rain – little ponds that become havens for insects, birds and amphibians.

Whenever I spot them, they always stop and stare back at me, ears pricked, their breath misting in the air. And then, just as quickly, they scatter – trotting off a short way before turning to check if I'm still there. Unlike the pigs, who come running at the first sound of footsteps, the ponies remain closer to their wild ancestors, always half-ready to move on.

Even their dung plays its part in the wider ecosystem, feeding beetles and worms, enriching the soil, and continuing the ancient cycle of life and decay. To watch the ponies is to glimpse a process as old as Britain's wild landscapes: the quiet, constant shaping of land by hoof and tooth.

BALANCE IN THE WILDLANDS

Together, the pigs and ponies form part of a tug of war between flora and fauna – between plants determined to dominate and animals determined to open space.

A Tamworth pig rootling within the rewilded landscape of the estate.

Left unchecked, thistles, docks or coarse grasses would crowd out more delicate species. But by grazing, rootling, browsing and producing dung, these animals keep everything in balance. It is not a manicured process; it is messy, seasonal and alive.

These are the real managers of the land, not us. We are simply the custodians, stepping back to allow them to do what their ancestors once did across Britain. And while they are cared for here – checked daily, moved to fresh ground when needed and given shelter when the weather turns really harsh – their lives are as close to wild as we can allow them.

Autumn may seem like a season of endings, but here it feels like preparation. The pigs and ponies are not winding down for winter but working harder than ever – disturbing soil, eating back growth, creating spaces. They are setting the land to rest, ensuring that when spring returns, it will come back richer, wilder and more abundant.

ABOVE An Exmoor pony roaming freely across the Wildlands.
OVERLEAF White Park cattle and Exmoor ponies grazing together across the Wildlands.

The 4th Earl, Scandal and Sandwiches

IF ONE MONTAGU ANCESTOR embodies both the grandeur and the scandal that so often run side by side in aristocratic history, it is John Montagu, 4th Earl of Sandwich (1718–1792). He was a man of contrasts: statesman, patron of the arts and sciences, naval reformer, devoted father, but also a notorious gambler and the man remembered, rather unfairly, for inventing the sandwich. His life reads almost like a stage play, and through the archives and portraits at Mapperton we catch intimate glimpses of the man behind the myth.

LETTERS THAT SPANNED AN AGE

In the Muniment Room we hold an extraordinary collection of the 4th Earl's papers, filling thirteen archive boxes. Altogether there are around 1,300 items, a correspondence that opens a window on to the cultural, political and personal life of eighteenth-century Britain. The names alone could be a syllabus in Enlightenment history. Sir Joseph Banks writes to him about scientific discovery. 'Capability' Brown and his son send reports from their travels and estates, including twenty letters full of politics, appointments and personal news. Astronomer Royal Nevil Maskelyne discusses plans for observing meteors. From the theatre comes David Garrick. From the world of music, Joah Bates, who masterminded the Handel Commemoration of 1784, writes twelve letters, joined by Charles Burney, the great music historian.

These are not dusty documents – they are living voices. Reading them, one can almost hear the hum of Georgian London: the debates, the discoveries, the performances. They remind us that Sandwich was more than a politician. He was part of the wider cultural movement of his age, exchanging thoughts with the leading minds of science and the arts.

LOVE, LOSS AND MARTHA RAY

The most poignant – and notorious – part of the archive is not the statesmanlike exchanges but the deeply personal. The 4th Earl's marriage collapsed early on and into this void stepped Martha Ray, a gifted singer. John and Martha's relationship lasted over fifteen years and produced several children. Nearly ninety papers in the collection relate to her, including seventeen of her own letters to Sandwich. They chart a story of affection and domestic partnership, as well as the precarious position of a woman who was neither wife nor free.

The tragedy came in April 1779 when Martha was murdered outside Covent Garden Theatre by a jealous lover. The scandal rocked London. The file of papers relating to her death is still among our boxes

After Johann Zoffany, portrait of John Montagu, 4th Earl of Sandwich.

at Mapperton – testimony to an event that shocked contemporaries as much as it moves us now.

Two portraits in our Drawing Room keep the pair side by side. On one wall hangs Sir Joshua Reynolds's 1758 portrait of the 4th Earl, standing proudly in his peer's robes. Next to him, in a work once attributed to Gainsborough, is Martha, seated, graceful and holding a fan. Their proximity in the room says something important: for all the gossip, the relationship mattered.

THE SANDWICH ISLANDS

The 4th Earl's name travelled further than any other in the family. When Captain James Cook charted the Pacific in the 1770s, he christened Hawaii the 'Sandwich Islands' in his honour. This part of the story strikes a very personal chord. I visited Hawaii in my youth, never imagining that those islands – so central to American identity today – once carried the name of my future husband's ancestor.

And the reach of Sandwich extended beyond the Pacific. Off the coast of Queensland, Australia, lies Hinchinbrook Island. (It's worth noting that there were variations on spelling then to what the family use now – Hichinbrook and Montague being examples.) Captain Cook first spotted it in 1770, naming it Mount Hinchinbrook after the family seat in Huntingdonshire, though he didn't realize at the time it was an island. Travelling with my family to Hinchinbrook Island was a moment I will never forget. Standing there, thousands of miles from Dorset, there was a strangeness to it: here we were on a tropical shore carrying the name of Hinchingbrooke, and for me, as an American who grew up with no sense of this history, it suddenly became real.

Nor did it stop there. Montagu Island in the South Sandwich Islands carries the same imprint. Each is a geographical thank you to the 4th Earl, whose support for exploration ensured that his name – and by extension, his family's – would be scattered like seeds on maps across the globe.

THE SANDWICH LEGACY

History remembers John Montagu, 4th Earl of Sandwich, in two very different ways. On the one hand, he was three times First Lord of the Admiralty, a reformer of the Navy, and a patron of exploration and the arts. On the other, his name has become forever linked to the humble sandwich. The story everyone knows is that he was a gambler who refused to leave the card table. Unwilling to get his hands greasy, he asked his butler to place a piece of meat between two slices of bread so that he could continue playing. It is a tale that has clung to him ever since, repeated in books, classrooms and kitchens across the world.

But in the family, we prefer – and believe – another version. The 4th Earl was not simply a gambler, but a diligent politician who often worked long hours at his desk. In the Staircase Hall at Mapperton hangs a portrait of him after Johann Zoffany showing Sandwich seated, papers in hand. It is an image of a statesman absorbed in his work, and we like to think this is the truer picture: a man too busy with affairs of government to break for a proper meal, improvising instead with bread and meat so as not to stain his documents. It is a small correction to a well-worn story, but one that matters.

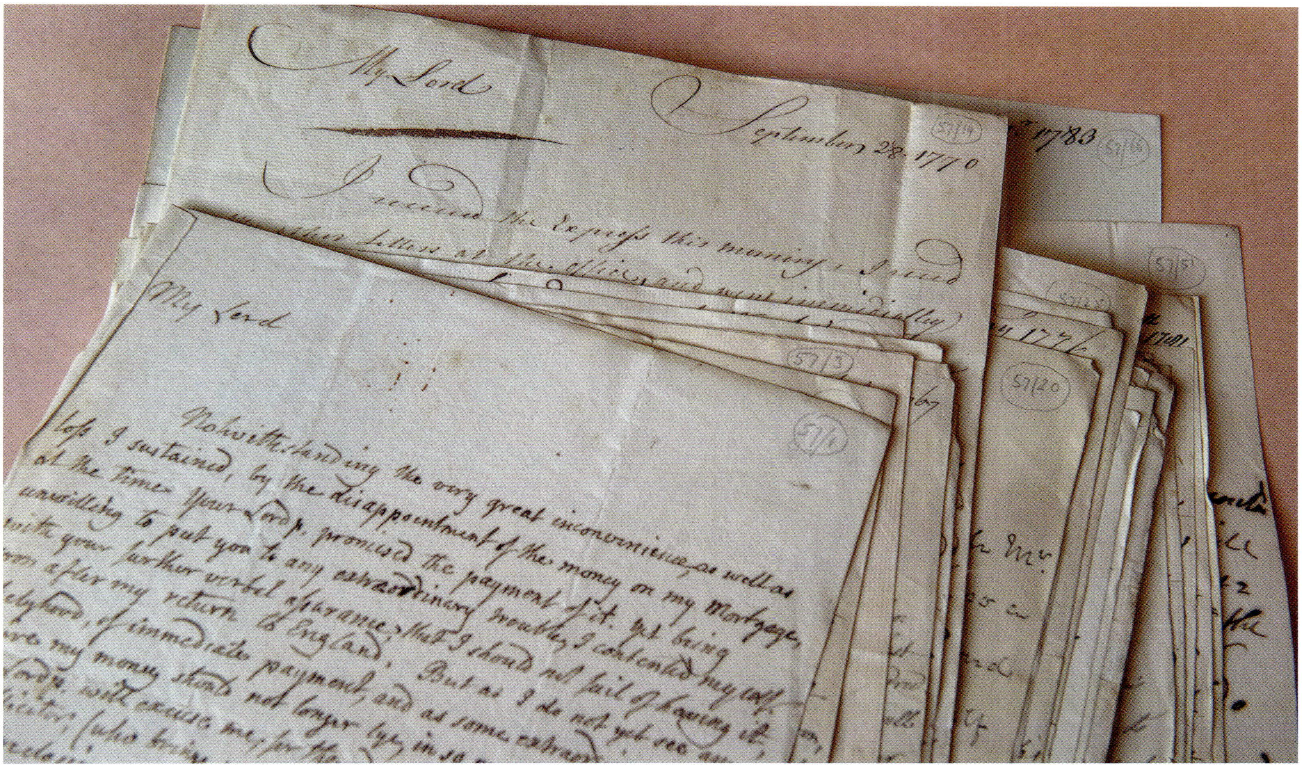

ABOVE Letters from the vast surviving correspondence of the 4th Earl of Sandwich, whose papers preserve an extraordinary record of eighteenth-century political, cultural and family life.

OVERLEAF (*left page*) Portrait of Captain James Cook, the celebrated navigator and explorer.. (*right page*) Portraits of the 4th Earl of Sandwich and Martha Ray, displayed together.

IACOVES COOK

SANDWICH'S VOYAGE
1799
SANDWICH'S VOYAGE
EARL OF SANDWICH'S VOYAGE
VOYAGES ROUND THE WORLD
VOL I
VOYAGES ROUND THE WORLD
VOL II

Travels, Textiles and Music

EACH SEASON AT Mapperton invites me to turn to different corners of its history. In autumn, when the rooms are quieter, I return again and again to the family collection. Here, in drawers and cupboards, behind glass and wrapped in tissue, are fragments of lives lived centuries before us. Three objects tell, in different ways, of John Montagu, 4th Earl of Sandwich – diplomat, traveller, patron of music – and a man whose private life was never far from public attention.

THE GRAND TOUR JOURNALS

I first came across the journals while dusting books in the Library. Two volumes caught my eye because they seemed to be falling apart – the spines were missing, the stitching exposed and the text block was holding together only by threads. At first glance I thought they simply needed repair. When I pulled them down and opened them, however, I realized how important they were: the original handwritten volumes recording the 4th Earl's Grand Tour of the 1730s. Though not penned by Sandwich himself, but by his scribe, the journals still bear his presence, with folded-in, pinned notes written in his own hand. They are absolutely stunning, though incredibly fragile, and since that discovery I've made their conservation one of my fundraising priorities.

The story the journals tell is unlike the usual Grand Tour diaries of the age. Fresh from Trinity College, Cambridge, John chose the unusual and the dangerous. He sailed far beyond the conventional route of Italy and France, travelling instead through Greece, Turkey and Egypt – all then within the Ottoman Empire. In Constantinople he immersed himself in the study of the language and customs, an experience that left a deep mark on him. When he returned to England a year later, he carried back not only the experience of travel in distant lands but also manuscripts, antiquities and ideas that astonished polite society. The journey gave him the reputation of a scholar-traveller, unusual among his peers, and later he channelled this curiosity into London's dining and learned societies.

In 1744, together with Francis Dashwood of West Wycombe, Buckinghamshire, he founded the Divan Club, a short-lived but remarkable Orientalist society for those who had travelled in the Ottoman Empire. For two years its members gathered over dinners to exchange stories, compare experiences and cultivate an interest in the East. The handwritten volumes I found in the library are the original source for much of this material. They were later printed under the title *A Voyage Performed by the Late Earl of Sandwich Round the Mediterranean in the Years 1738 and 1739*, a first edition of which we also keep in the Library. Yet nothing compares to the fragile beauty of the originals, with their missing spines and exposed stitching, which make the past feel so close.

The 4th Earl of Sandwich's Grand Tour journals, their damaged bindings revealing centuries of use and survival.

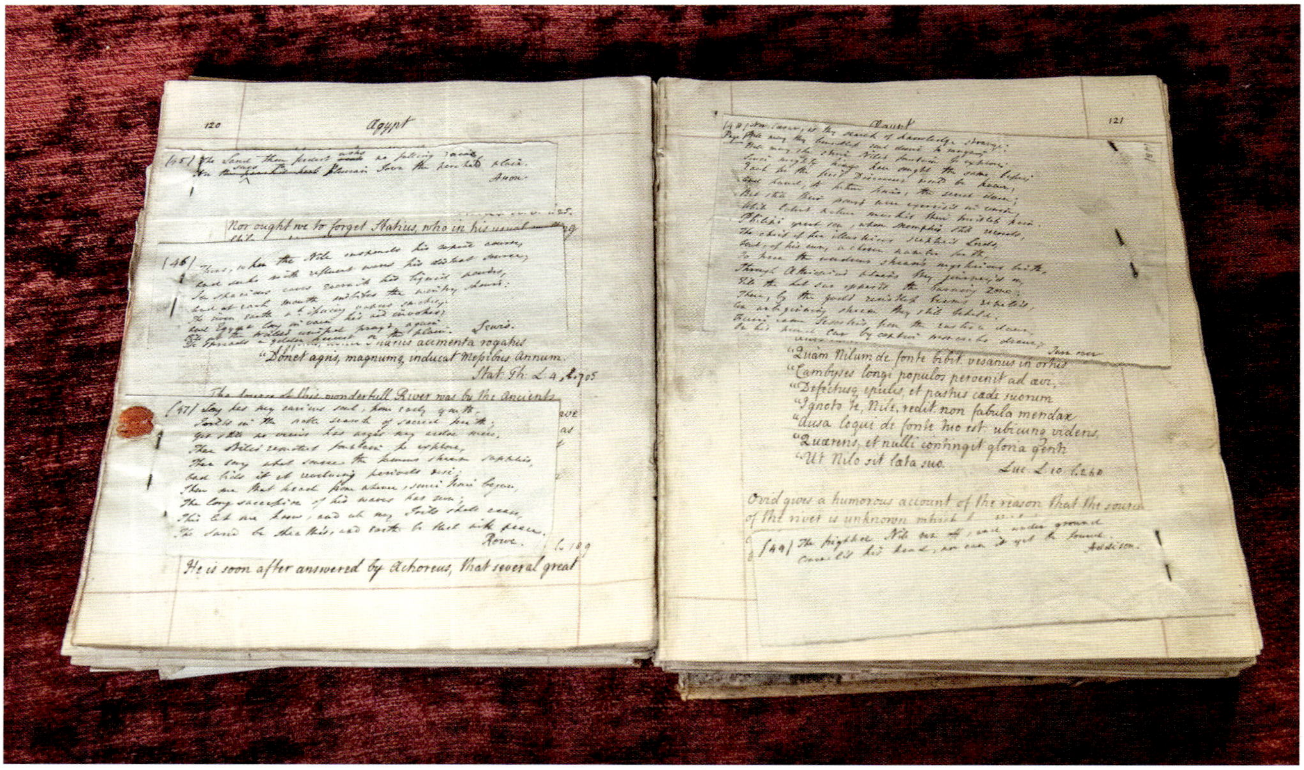
120
Aegypt
121

VIII
20
POST
PORTUM
TOT NAUFRAGIA
Montagu, Earl of Sandwich
Viscount Hinchinbroke &c.

OVERTURES
TYMPANO

HANDEL, THE BIRDS AND MISS RAY'S MUSIC

The volumes of music once owned by Martha are quieter but no less evocative. Bound in calf or in fine red morocco, they contain the works of Handel – *Jephtha*, *Samson*, *Saul* and the *Coronation Anthems* – alongside Dieupart's *Six Suittes de Clavessin*. Several of the bindings bear the name 'Miss Ray' on the cover, a rare and intimate mark of ownership. These were not books to be left untouched on a shelf; they were made to be played, and they remind us of Martha's own career as a singer. She rose to prominence in London during the later years of Handel's life, performing in the oratorios and operas that dominated the city's theatres. After Handel's death in 1759 she continued to be a leading soprano in the London oratorio scene, where his music was still frequently performed.

In our archive she is described as gentle and lovable, devoted to Lord Sandwich, and admired even by his legitimate children. She spoke several languages and was considered a gifted musician; her manuscript music, madrigals, glees and songs were long preserved at Hinchingbrooke. She was also a great lover of birds. The Central Hall there once housed an aviary with species from across the world, and the artist William Hayes painted them, creating delicate pictures. These works, once at Hinchingbrooke, are now here at Mapperton, offering a glimpse into Martha's world.

FACING (*top*) The 4th Earl of Sandwich's Grand Tour journal, with his annotations and inserted notes. (*bottom left*) A bookplate indicating ownership by the 4th Earl of Sandwich. (*bottom right*) A volume from Miss Ray's music collection, preserved at Mapperton and still retaining its original marbled paper boards. RIGHT (*top*) Handel's signature on one of the music volumes from Martha Ray's collection. (*bottom*) Julie reflected in the Staircase Hall's mirror, framed by William Haye's paintings of Martha's beloved birds.

Bound volumes of Handel's music from the collection belonging to Martha Ray.

MISS: RAY
OVERTURES
TYMPANO
Jephtha
an
Oratorio,
IN SCORE
Composed by
M^r. HANDEL.
with
His Additional Quintetto
L O N D O N
Printed for Willm. Randall, Succefsor to the late M^r.
J. Walsh, in Catharine Street in the Strand. Of Whom
may be had, the Compleat Scores of Mefsiah, Samson,
Judas Maccabaeus, & L'Allegro Il Pensoroso.

MARTHA RAY'S GOWN

When my mother-in-law first showed me this dress, I was absolutely gobsmacked. It is so stunning that even in its fragile state it takes your breath away. The robe, which with strong probability once belonged to Martha Ray, is a sack-backed open gown in brocaded silk. The French fabric, woven in Lyons between 1730 and 1740, is extraordinary. Against its ivory background, curling silver and blue leaves intertwine with scarlet blossoms and rose hips in green and silver. Yet the weight of the brocade has strained its seams; the shoulders have begun to weaken; the hem is cut and recut; the petticoat pieced together from panels and patches. Time, fashion and nineteenth-century alteration have all left their mark. Still, when you stand before it, it is easy to picture Martha in her prime, the box pleats at the back falling perfectly, the silk catching the light of the theatre lamps. It is a garment that speaks of both splendour and fragility, as if her story is still stitched into the fabric.

ABOVE A sack-backed open gown in brocaded Lyon silk, c.1730–1740.
FACING Detail of the silk brocade, with silver and blue foliage, scarlet blossoms and green rose hips woven against an ivory ground.

Medmenham Abbey and the Hellfire Caves, Lord Sandwich's Circle

WHEN I FIRST BEGAN researching the 4th Earl, I thought I understood the broad outline of his life: an accomplished politician, a long-serving naval administrator, the man who supported Captain Cook's voyages, and of course the man who lent his name to that enduring staple of modern life – the sandwich. But as with so many ancestors, once you start digging deeper you uncover other layers. And in John Montagu's case, one of those layers is both surprising and, frankly, rather shocking. Because alongside his public career, the 4th Earl was part of one of the most notorious circles of Georgian England: the so-called Hellfire Club.

Their story begins not in Westminster, but on the banks of the Thames at Medmenham Abbey in Buckinghamshire. Today it is a private house in a picturesque riverside setting, but in the eighteenth century Sir Francis Dashwood transformed its ruins into a Gothic fantasy. Further north, on the slopes of West Wycombe Hill, visitors today can also walk through the Hellfire Caves, a remarkable network of tunnels open to the public, which were once the subterranean stage for the same circle's activities.

Medmenham Abbey had once been a quiet Cistercian house, dissolved in the sixteenth century, but under Dashwood it was refashioned as the perfect setting for mischief. Above the entrance he placed the motto 'Do what thou wilt'. Within its walls, his companions styled themselves as 'Monks of Medmenham', adopting mock titles, donning robes and parodying sacred rituals with irreverent humour. And our ancestor, the 4th Earl of Sandwich, was among them.

It is still startling to reconcile: on one side, a man serving as First Lord of the Admiralty, hosting great figures of the age; and on the other, a 'Brother' in Dashwood's circle, donning monkish robes, parodying religious rituals and indulging in revels that scandalized the neighbourhood. For all the elegance of the Georgian interiors at Mapperton and other Montagu houses, here was a very different use of architecture – ruins transformed into theatres of irreverence.

The Abbey, however, soon became too conspicuous. Rumours abounded along the Thames of what went on inside. Some stories were exaggerated, no doubt, but others were probably near the truth: heavy drinking, raucous banquets, pagan symbolism and a mischievous delight in pushing boundaries. To escape the growing scrutiny, Dashwood and his circle went underground – quite literally.

Between 1748 and 1752, he commissioned the excavation of a series of tunnels beneath West Wycombe Hill. Officially, the work was to provide chalk for road building and employment for local men.

Medmenham Abbey, Buckinghamshire, associated with the 4th Earl of Sandwich.

In reality, it produced the Hellfire Caves – a sprawling underground complex, complete with chambers given names like Whitehead's Cave (after the poet Paul Whitehead), Franklin's Cave (after Benjamin Franklin, who visited Dashwood), and most intriguingly of all, Lord Sandwich's Circle. Yes, even in the darkness of those passages, our ancestor's name was inscribed into the geography of the caves.

At the centre lay the Banqueting Hall, where great feasts were held, and beyond a subterranean river – tellingly called the Styx – was the Inner Temple, directly beneath the parish church on the hilltop. There, amid flickering candlelight, the club's most secretive rituals were staged.

It is hard not to be fascinated by the duality of it all. The same man who was helping steer Britain's navy through turbulent waters, who was a loyal partner to the singer Martha Ray, and who has gone down in history for a simple but ingenious way of eating lunch – was also descending into these candlelit tunnels, part of a world designed for secrecy, satire and excess.

For me, these walls and tunnels highlight one of the most intriguing things about family history: the way ancestors refuse to be one-dimensional. The 4th Earl was not just a politician, not just a reformer, not just the man behind the sandwich. He was also a participant in one of the era's most infamous societies, his name forever attached to a lunchtime snack as well as a candlelit chamber deep beneath a Buckinghamshire hill.

John Montagu, 4th Earl of Sandwich.

Winter

There's something rather wonderful about Mapperton in winter. No bustle of visitors, no dodging of tours through the house, no chatter in the Coach House – just a quiet estate and a slower rhythm. With the gates closed for the season, the house, the gardens and the Wildlands all take a long breath. The gravel drive is empty, the cafe doors are locked, and even the Exmoor ponies seem to settle into a softer pace. For me, it's when Mapperton feels most like home.

That's not to say it's restful. Quite the opposite – now is the time when all the behind-the-scenes work begins. You simply can't polish oak panelling or move antique furniture when people are walking through the rooms every hour. So, I get to work. The panelling in the Hall always needs a proper clean, and let me tell you, it absolutely soaks up months of summer dust. The overmantel in the West Room is too delicate for a cloth – it's a dry sponge only, very gently. And yes, I still hold my breath doing it.

Whether it's gently mending the leg of a Georgian side table or dusting off one of the journals in the Library, winter is when I get things done. Sometimes, just for a change of pace, I rearrange a few pictures, seeing if I can spark a new conversation between works that have been politely ignoring each other for far too long. And then there's the glitter – from Christmas, I mean – which somehow manages to reappear in June. Meanwhile, the rest of the house requires its own kind of tending. Winter is no time to slack: pipes have to be watched, draughts blocked, fires lit.

But my favourite winter ritual lies in the archives. I head into the Muniment Room in fingerless gloves and a woolly hat – always – and settle in beside the scanner with a strong cup of herbal tea. This is a house built to keep the cool in, which is wonderful in August but far less welcome in February. I've even been spotted sitting on top of the Aga just to thaw out. But despite the cold, the archives are where I lose all track of time. Digitizing and reading Luke's great-grandmother Alberta's letters, there's this uncanny sense of companionship – as if she's just stepped out of the room and left a note on the desk.

Although the house itself is closed to day visitors in winter, the estate is briefly and joyfully thrown open again for our busiest – and most festive – event of the year: the Mapperton Christmas Market. Always held over two days on the weekend after Thanksgiving (I still carry that very American instinct that Christmas should not properly begin before then), it draws thousands of people back through the gates. More than a hundred local craftspeople fill the Coach House cafe and courtyards with stalls, while mulled wine and mince pies flow freely, live bands play outside and Father Christmas holds court in his grotto. For those

Winter view of the pools and landscape.

two days, the winter quiet gives way to music, laughter and community, and for me it is a wonderful way to welcome everyone back into the estate before the year gently draws to a close.

Decorating the house for Christmas has become its own tradition. When I first moved to England, I had no idea what swags were – I soon learned. Now we go out and forage on the estate for holly, mistletoe, pine cones, coloured berries and all sorts of winter greenery. We make big, bold swags for the doorways of rooms that we'll actually use over the holidays: the Dining Room, the Hall and the Staircase Hall. Then there's the holly – we place small sprigs above portraits of past Montagus so that, as we always say, they can celebrate Christmas with us.

The garland on the main staircase is one of my favourite decorations. It's a tradition I started with my sister-in-law a few years ago, made using ivy and cuttings from the garden. It winds its way along the banister – and the effect is truly spectacular. It takes me about six hours to make, but it's worth every minute.

Each December, we also hold a carol concert for the local community in the church. Afterwards, everyone walks back to the house and into the Hall for mulled wine and mince pies in front of the fire. And then, of course, there's Christmas lunch – a big family affair with all the trimmings. There are party poppers, a flaming Christmas pudding, the usual terrible cracker jokes, and those little gold and silver paper crowns that somehow stay on through pudding and washing up.

LEFT (*top and bottom*) Rehinging and hanging pictures in the Dining Room as part of seasonal care of the collection.
FACING Cleaning eighteenth-century Japanned screens, part of the ongoing conservation of Mapperton's interiors.

Outside, the gardens settle into themselves. It's the time of year when their structure really shows: the bones of the design, the paths, the topiary. The wisteria is bare, the pergola clear, the pools are black mirrors. And if we're lucky enough to get snow – just a sprinkling – for a moment Mapperton becomes a Christmas card come to life. The Wildlands, too, feel changed. There's less movement, of course, but you can see more: the shape of the land, the way the trees mark the sky.

As my father-in-law once said, 'You have to have a lot of energy and entrepreneurial flair.' And that's especially true in winter. The house might look asleep, but underneath it all there's planning, cleaning, mending, planting, dreaming.

Winter at Mapperton isn't grand. It's not showy. But it is peaceful. It's when the house gets to rest, and so do we – at least a little. There's a quietness here, a sort of exhale, before the whole cycle begins again. And standing in the middle of it, you can feel just how far we've come and how ready we'll be, come spring, to open the doors once more.

ABOVE The house illuminated against the winter darkness.
FACING Julie in the Dining Room.
OVERLEAF Mapperton House in winter.

The Church and Muniment Room

THE CHURCH AT MAPPERTON doesn't sit apart from the house in a distant field, as many country house churches do. It's pressed right up against the West Front of the manor, its ancient Ham stone walls forming one continuous thread of architecture with the house itself. And in winter, when the gardens are quiet, the trees are bare and the landscape withdraws into itself, the church becomes one of the most atmospheric places on the estate.

All Saints Church has stood here in some form since at least the thirteenth century. The original church would have been small, likely built of stone rubble and timber, serving the manor and the village. Its shape and footprint have changed over time, but its purpose has not: it has remained, throughout the centuries, a place for both the sacred and the domestic to meet.

The most significant transformation came in the seventeenth century. Richard Brodrepp II turned his attention to the church as part of his broader efforts to modernize and unify the estate, and rebuilt the nave, giving it the layout and classical simplicity we see today. Brodrepp's design achieved a restrained, classically proportioned space that echoed his other improvements to the manor. In other words, he succeeded in making the church feel like part of the house.

It's the architectural harmony that makes All Saints Church so unique. The building is not a showpiece, nor is it grand. Instead, it's compact, grounded and utterly integrated into the rhythm of the manor. The building invites you in without ceremony. You open the wooden door and step into cool stone stillness.

Inside, the nave is quietly elegant, but it's in the stained glass that the church really begins to speak. Set into the otherwise plain windows are over sixty small panels – roundels and decorative fragments – that shimmer in the low winter light. They are a striking mix of English and Continental glass from the sixteenth and seventeenth centuries.

At the tops of the windows sit a series of colourful heraldic roundels, likely salvaged from earlier buildings or brought here during restorations. At least one is believed to have come from the original Hall, when the Morgan family lived here in the sixteenth century. Beneath the roundels are smaller panels of painted glass, many of which were imported in the eighteenth century but are of sixteenth century origin, from what we now call Belgium and the Netherlands, a region then known as the Low Countries, and famous for its glass painting. Some of the panels depict scenes from scripture, while others are purely decorative, but together they create a gentle mosaic of ruby red, cobalt

The entrance to All Saints Church integrated directly into Mapperton House.

blue, amber and gold that animates the stone around it. These panels were brought together gradually and what survives today is a glowing collage of faith, family and the fashionable tastes of past centuries.

The carol service tradition was started by my in-laws in the 1980s when they moved to Mapperton, and it has continued ever since. We don't promote it widely – it is really for the village and the wider estate community – but somehow, every year, the pews fill. The church is heated now, thanks to the biomass boiler we installed on the estate a decade ago, but most people still wear coats, scarves and woolly hats. The cold tends to hang around the stone floor. But when the first few notes of 'Once in Royal David's City' rise up through the nave, the temperature suddenly seems irrelevant. You can imagine generations of Brodrepps, Comptons and Montagus sitting here before us, singing the very same carols in the very same place.

After the final hymn, most people take the path around to the front of the house, heading towards the Hall where warmth and mulled wine await. But I tend to slip through a different route: a small door that connects the church to the house via the Muniment Room.

FACING Heraldic rondels in stained glass within All Saints Church.
ABOVE (*left*) A heraldic glass roundel in All Saints Church.
(*right*) Sixteenth-century painted glass panel.

This connecting corridor was never part of the original manor, but rather a modest early twentieth-century addition. It was built simply to allow the family to move between house and church without getting wet – a charming walk in summer, but far less appealing in December. Today, we call this room the Muniment Room. But it wasn't always so.

The word 'muniment' comes from the Latin *munimentum*, meaning a 'fortification' or 'defence', extended to describe documentary defences for property – appropriate for a place that now guards over some of the most vital documents in the Sandwich family story. In Ethel Labouchere's time, in the early twentieth century, it served as a sitting room for the servants. It wasn't built with archives in mind.

Now, though, it's my sanctuary.

When I first stepped into the Muniment Room in earnest in 2023 – having just discovered Alberta's astonishing collection of nearly ten thousand letters – it was in a rather sorry state. Damp streaked the walls, the ceiling was stained and it was very cold. The documents were a bit scattered. There was no system or preservation strategy.

So I launched a restoration project. I started reading Alberta's letters aloud every week on our 'Mapperton Live!' YouTube channel, beginning in early 2023. People were fascinated – not just by her words, but by the sheer scope and intimacy of the archive. Viewers began sending in donations via YouTube, which made me realize that if we set up a proper fundraiser, we might be able to do something amazing.

I launched the campaign through a crowdfunding platform, and the support was overwhelming. Donors received digital certificates signed by both me and Alberta (I carefully copied her signature). I made bookmarks and postcards from scanned images of Alberta's letters and her handwritten recipes from her book of receipts (more on that later), and sent them out to contributors. For those who gave significant amounts, we engraved their names on to a brass and walnut plaque – now mounted on the wall of the Muniment Room – so that a hundred years from now, anyone walking into this room will know exactly who helped to bring it to life.

And then something unexpected happened. While repositioning one of the bookcases to allow better access to a corner of the archive, we uncovered a hidden seventeenth-century window – an original exterior window that had once looked out on to the front courtyard before the corridor was built. For a brief moment, it felt like time folded back on itself.

Today, the Muniment Room has three doors. One leads directly into the church. Another connects to a back corridor in the house. And the third – almost a secret door – opens into what is now the Dining Room. In every way, it's a room of thresholds: between sacred and domestic, between past and present, between story and archive.

The archive itself now stretches neatly across the room: labelled box files sorted by decade and family name from the 4th Earl of Sandwich to the present day. Alberta's letters are carefully housed here, alongside family photo albums, journals, estate ledgers and legal documents.

A Chippendale desk from Hinchingbrooke sits between two bookcases and it is here that I work,

The nave of All Saints Church, rebuilt in the seventeenth century by Richard Brodrepp II.

Alberta
Roseti
297 Fifth Ave., N. Y.

scanning letters (with the help of volunteers), uploading digital backups, and quietly building an online archive out of fragile ink and paper.

Sometimes, I retreat here when the rest of the house is busy. I sit at the desk, surrounded by history, and feel very fortunate. This room isn't grand, but it's important. It holds stories. And I feel, in some small way, that it has become a beating pulse of the house again.

But on carol service night, I don't linger long. There are mince pies to warm and mulled wine to stir, and the Hall is already starting to fill and the windows glowing from within. The fire is blazing. It's the most natural, grounded moment of the season – nothing staged, just community.

The evening always seems to flow effortlessly – from ancient stone and stained glass, to archive shelves and digital scans, to the crackle of the firelight and the clink of glasses. Three spaces, three centuries, bound by continuity and care.

FACING *(top left)* Julie, Caroline and John sorting files in the archive room prior to redecoration. *(top right)* Alberta Sturges, aged 17, 1894. *(bottom left)* Discovered behind a repositioned bookcase, this hidden seventeenth-century window was once an exterior opening looking onto the front courtyard. *(bottom right)* The reorganised archive shelves of the Muniment Room. ABOVE A Chippendale desk from Hinchingbrooke House now in the Muniment Room.

Orangery and Statuary

WINTER AT MAPPERTON is a season I've come to treasure. The gardens lose their bright colour and fullness, yes – but what emerges is something quieter, more architectural and, in many ways, more revealing. With the trees bare and the flower beds resting, the framework of the garden reveals itself. You begin to see the bones of the place – the lines of the terraces, the old stone walls softened by moss, the deep structure of the yew topiary, the way everything folds gently into the valley.

Even as the landscape rests, there are still signs of life. The first snowdrops begin to appear: small and determined, scattered through the banks and borders like quiet punctuation marks. Winter aconites bloom along the red wall in a cheerful blaze of yellow. Colchicums – autumn-flowering crocus – hold their ground along the grey wall. Under the pergola, hellebores and epimediums begin to show in late January and February, their colours subtle but unmistakably hopeful. It's as if the garden is taking a deep breath – not asleep, just gathering itself for what's next.

At the top of the gardens stands a striking iron gate topped with an earl's coronet. It wasn't always here at Mapperton. The gate was brought down from Hinchingbrooke, as a reminder of the Montagus' long journey. Even now, darkened by time and weather, the gate stands proud as a small but significant link between past and present.

Just beyond that gate is one of my favourite winter spots: the Orangery. It was built by Victor Montagu, my husband's grandfather, in 1968. Perched at the top of the Fountain Court, the Orangery offers one of the most wonderful views down the length of the garden. Its creation marked perhaps the most significant change Victor made to the garden landscape. He removed a nineteenth-century glasshouse that had fallen into disrepair and replaced it with something entirely new: a building that felt both classical and practical, and completely at home in its surroundings. Victor had a clear vision – he wanted a place to sit, either inside or out, and take in the gardens in all seasons, even when it was too cold to linger outdoors.

The Orangery was built using Minster reconstituted stone, and over time it has weathered so naturally into its surroundings that many visitors assume it's an original eighteenth-century feature. The architecture is simple and well proportioned, with tall windows that catch the low winter sun and fill the space with light. In winter, the orangery houses a mix of tender and interesting plants – including clivias, tree ferns, an avocado, a grape vine, birds of paradise and banana plants. It's not a display house as such, but more a

FACING Winter lays bare the structure of the Italianate garden.
OVERLEAF In winter, the clipped architecture of the Italianate garden comes fully into view.

working space that keeps these more delicate plants protected through the colder months. And yet, despite its practicality, it remains one of the loveliest places to pause. On a crisp winter morning, with frost glinting on the lawns and sunlight streaming through the glass, the Orangery feels like a quiet refuge.

None of what we see today would have been possible without the work that came before, and Mapperton had needed that work. Mrs Labouchere had laid the early foundations – placing ornaments, establishing paths and planting – but by the time Victor and my in-laws arrived, the place needed energy, vision and a good deal of care. They brought all three.

The Orangery itself has needed its own care over the years. Most recently, we restored the windows. The frames had weathered badly, and several panes were cracked, loose or missing. We restored them carefully, making sure to retain the original look while giving the structure back its strength.

There's something deeply satisfying about the history of orangeries. They first appeared in Renaissance Italy, built by wealthy families to protect citrus trees from frost. But they were never just practical; they were places to linger, to enjoy the garden in winter light. By the seventeenth century, they'd become fashionable additions to great English estates. Mapperton's Orangery continues that tradition: not to show off, but to settle into the rhythm of the landscape. It's not grand, but it's rooted. It feels like it's always been here.

All around the garden in winter, sculptures begin to come into focus. In summer, they're often tucked behind greenery or half-hidden by leaves. But in winter, they stand out – gently marking paths, anchoring corners or just waiting to be discovered. Mrs Labouchere had a particular passion for bird and animal statuary. She built up a collection that's still scattered throughout the grounds, softened now by time and cloaked in a beautiful patina of moss and lichen.

Most of her pieces are made from cast concrete or reconstituted stone – materials that were quite innovative in the 1920s. They allowed for detailed forms that weathered well and could be produced affordably. At one end of the garden, a lichen-speckled heron stands sentry, as if keeping watch over the changing seasons. Ethel had an eye for placement,

LEFT One of the Orangery's original windows, framed by stonework carved with the Montagu lozenges.
FACING The interior of the Orangery in winter.

ABOVE Two of Mrs Labouchere's heron sculptures keeps watch above the terraces.

ABOVE (*left*) An owl from Mrs Labouchere's collection of garden statuary, its weathered surface softened by decades of moss and lichen. (*right*) Winter brings Mapperton's statuary into sharper focus.

and this one, like so many others, feels exactly right where it is.

There are others, too: urns with softened outlines, neoclassical figures tucked into sheltered alcoves, an owl, a lion peering over the Fountain Court. These figures don't demand attention, but they become more visible in winter, standing out more clearly against the bare hedges and frosted lawns.

And just when you think the garden has gone completely quiet, the snowdrops arrive. Each February, they begin to push up through the cold ground – simple, elegant and hopeful. They are the first real sign that winter is starting to give way. We open the gardens for special days to celebrate them. It's always lovely to see people spotting new patches of white and green where none had been the week before.

Mapperton in winter may not be showy, but it's deeply atmospheric. There's a stillness to it, but not a silence. It's a time of rest, but also of quiet preparation. Beneath the frozen ground and bare branches, life is still happening. The garden is storing up its energy for spring. And I think that's what I love most about this time of year – it's a reminder that growth can come out of stillness, and that even the most dormant seasons have their own kind of vitality.

ABOVE The Orangery at the top of the Fountain Court, built by Victor Montagu in 1968, replacing a derelict Victorian glasshouse with a structure designed to sit naturally within the landscape.
FACING A gate from Hinchingbrooke House bearing the earl's coronet, now at Mapperton.

William Montagu

VISCOUNT HINCHINGBROOKE

When my husband and I took over running the estate in 2016, Will was just eleven. He didn't grow up here, but over the years he's come to know the place well – helping with events, getting involved with rewilding, and slowly beginning to understand what it means to inherit not just a house, but everything that comes with it. I wanted to feature his voice because, while we're the current custodians, he's the future.

JULIE Will, thank you for sitting down with me. I know this might feel a bit strange, but I really wanted to include your thoughts in this book. To start with a big question: how do you feel about the importance of preserving British heritage? Does that resonate with you?

WILL I think as I've gotten older, it definitely resonates more. When I was younger, I probably didn't really appreciate the importance of keeping this part of history alive, but watching you and Dad over the years and how much work and care you've put into Mapperton, I've started to understand that more. But I think it's equally about keeping British heritage interesting and relevant in today's world and opening it up to a wider audience, as you've both been able to do so well through YouTube.

JULIE That leads nicely into the next question. Mapperton has so many layers – the house and its contents, the wider estate, the Wildlands, the gardens. Is there any particular part that you're especially interested in right now?

WILL There are many but I'd say the Wildlands project really interests me. It is fun and exciting and is doing a lot of good for the local biodiversity – on another note, I am just very fond of the pigs. I'm also interested in the restoration work, especially things that maybe haven't been a top priority over the years, like the tapestries. But what's really exciting to me is having the chance to bring in my personal interests to Mapperton, and for me that's music. There are already so many events here, such as the Dorset food and drink market and the plant fair, so I think a music and arts fair would be a great addition.

JULIE Music is such a big part of your life. Can you share a little more about that for the reader?

WILL Well, I've been playing guitar since around the age of nine. During COVID I was playing for maybe six hours a day, primarily as a way to keep me sane back then. After school, I went to music college for a year, so it's been a very big part of my life so far. We do have occasional concerts here, but it'd be great to find more ways of bringing music into the larger Mapperton scene.

JULIE Now I want to shift to something a bit more historical. Growing up, when did you realize you were part of a family with a long and storied history – that the 1st Earl of Sandwich helped bring Charles II back from exile, and that the title you'll one day inherit carries all of that weight?

WILL I don't think there was any big moment of realization because it has always been there, and so it's just felt familiar. There was never really any sense of disbelief about it. Yes, it's all quite unusual, but I don't think about it too much on a day-to-day basis, or else it would become overwhelming. What I would say is that I've come to understand and appreciate the family's heritage and history more as I've gotten older, and I'm sure that will continue.

JULIE And how do you feel about the idea that one day Mapperton will fall to you? I promise not to make this heavy!

WILL Most of the time I just try not to think about it, but in the back of my mind there's obviously a sense of responsibility. This has been your life, and Dad's and my grandparents' and so on, so I do feel that weight. But at the same time, I know I'll probably want to do things a bit differently and bring in my own ideas, as every generation does. I'm sure I'll think about what that might look like as I get older.

JULIE Finally, when you think of Mapperton, what's a memory or space that brings you the most joy?

WILL There are a lot but probably playing card games with my grandparents, John and Caroline. It has been something that I've always looked forward to and always enjoyed – even when losing – and I've felt very fortunate to have been able to spend so much time with them both. And, of course, bonfires with John. When I was younger, we would go out into the woods somewhere on the estate and build these great big bonfires, although I would often pile on too much wood and end up smothering the fire.

JULIE That's such a lovely memory to end on. Thank you, Will.

The Beavers' Silent Work

WINTER IS A SLOWER time at the Mapperton Wildlands. The days are shorter, the ground stays wet and most of the visible growth has stopped. But beneath the surface, the landscape is still changing, and some of the most important work begins at this time of year. If spring at Mapperton is a soft unfurling, winter is a quiet gathering in.

And tucked away in the Wildlands, in the hidden curves of an ancient woodland, a pair of beavers are doggedly changing everything. The beavers, absent from England for four hundred years, have returned to Mapperton. Their arrival is more than symbolic; it marks the beginning of a profound, natural transformation.

We first welcomed our beaver pair – a 15-kg (33-lb) male and a 20-kg (44-lb) female – to the estate in late autumn 2022, releasing them into a 3.2-ha (8-acre) enclosure carefully constructed in a stretch of ancient woodland. By the time winter settled over the valley, they had already begun the slow, determined work that would, in time, reshape the landscape. It was a season of small, patient gestures: a branch dragged here, a mud bank built there, channels cleared and shallow ponds formed as the water found new ways to move.

There is a humility about watching beavers at work, especially in winter. Unlike the urgent scramble of spring or the riotous flourishing of summer, their presence is a lesson in quiet persistence. Beneath the skeleton trees, where the ground is sodden and the air smells of damp earth and woodsmoke, they are rebuilding a lost world.

Four centuries ago, Britain's wetlands were bustling, layered places, knitted together by creatures like the beaver. When they disappeared – hunted out for their fur and for the medicinal use of their castoreum (the strong-smelling secretion from a beaver's castor sacs, near the tail) – it wasn't just a loss of one species, but the loss of a whole ecological engine. Waterways straightened, floodplains dried out, biodiversity withered. The land grew quieter.

Now, in the short days of winter, the Mapperton Wildlands are growing noisier again, if you know how to listen. The streams murmur over fresh dams; the banks are scored with the sharp wedge tracks of beaver teeth; and here and there, a newly felled tree leans across the water. At first glance, it all looks accidental. But stand long enough in the cold to watch and you see the intent, the order. Everything they do has purpose.

The Mapperton beavers are securely enclosed and the benefits, even in those early months, are visible. Where water once rushed away after heavy rain, it now pools and lingers. The wetlands hold it back, releasing it slowly, reducing the risk of flooding downstream – an extraordinary gift in a century where extreme weather

The beaver enclosure within the estate, part of Mapperton's rewilding programme.

is becoming the norm. Sediment, once carried away to clog rivers and streams, now settles quietly behind their dams. And though winter keeps the wild flowers and dragonflies in check, we know they will return to the new ponds and wet meadows come the warmer months.

When the beavers arrived, their first priority was to build a lodge. They waste nothing. Branches stripped of bark, carefully woven roots, mud meticulously packed into place – everything bears the unmistakable signature of their touch. And deep within the thick, muddy walls, the beavers sleep through the coldest days, venturing out only at dusk or dawn to gather food and maintain their expanding kingdom.

Rewilding is not about spectacle. It is about patience, about trust in the slow, natural processes we have so often tried to control or erase. Watching the beavers at this time of year – or, more often, noticing their work without seeing them at all – is a reminder that profound change rarely announces itself with trumpets. It begins in simple, careful gestures, unnoticed by most, until suddenly the whole landscape is new.

Luke and I often speak about how the Mapperton Wildlands is as much about *letting go* as it is about *doing*. Inspired by the rewilding successes at Knepp, we are learning to trust the land (see page 61). The beavers, without a blueprint or a grant application in sight, know exactly how to do it.

Their return is not merely a restoration of a missing species. It is a reawakening of a way of being, a restitching of the ancient fabric of life that once covered this valley.

FACING AND ABOVE Beavers within their wetland habitat in the Wildlands. OVERLEAF Early morning mist rising over the Wildlands at Mapperton.

Alberta Sturges, an Heiress Rediscovered

THE JOURNEY TO UNCOVER the life of Alberta Sturges (1877–1951), an American heiress who became the 9th Countess of Sandwich in 1916, began with a single painting. The first time I heard of Alberta was when my father-in-law pointed to a portrait hanging in the Staircase Hall, a striking piece by society painter Ambrose McEvoy. 'That is my grandmother,' he said casually, 'she was an American.' That single sentence was the start of a deep and enduring fascination, though at first I had little more than a name and a face to go on.

Alberta was one of many American heiresses who crossed the Atlantic in the late nineteenth and early twentieth centuries, part of a wave of women whose wealth helped to sustain and restore many great British estates. But unlike the more public figures of the Gilded Age – women like Consuelo Vanderbilt, Duchess of Marlborough, or Jennie Jerome, Winston Churchill's mother – Alberta's life wasn't lived entirely in the spotlight. Her legacy is quieter, more reflective and in many ways more intimate, because she left us her voice.

Years after being introduced to her portrait, as I delved into the archives, Alberta's life began to unfold before me. Through her thousands of letters, she spoke directly to me – and to history – offering a rare and personal glimpse into the life of a Gilded Age heiress.

We share more than a fascination with history, Alberta and I. Like her, I was born in Illinois and we were both drawn to yoga as a means of self-discovery and discipline. Yoga has been an integral part of my life for over twenty-five years, and Alberta's connection to Swami Vivekananda, the Hindu monk and philosopher, resonates deeply with me. His teachings inspired Alberta to explore spiritual practices that were groundbreaking for her time, much as yoga continues to shape my own path today.

Alberta's portrait has a commanding presence and it remained in my thoughts long after my father-in-law's casual introduction. Who was this woman? How did she, an American, find her way into the Montagu family? Initially, my questions yielded few answers. The family's knowledge of Alberta's background was vague, even reticent, as if her story had been tucked away, much like the archives in the Muniment Room where her letters were hidden.

It wasn't until I pursued and subsequently completed a Master's degree in Country House Studies that I truly began to unravel her life. I chose Alberta as the subject of my dissertation, a decision driven by curiosity and the desire to give her voice a platform. The archives, or Muniment Room, became my second home during this period.

In the Muniment Room, amid box files, Alberta's story began to emerge. Her letters, thousands of them, written in her slanted late nineteenth-century hand,

Portrait of Alberta Sturges, April 1905.

HINCHINGBROOKE

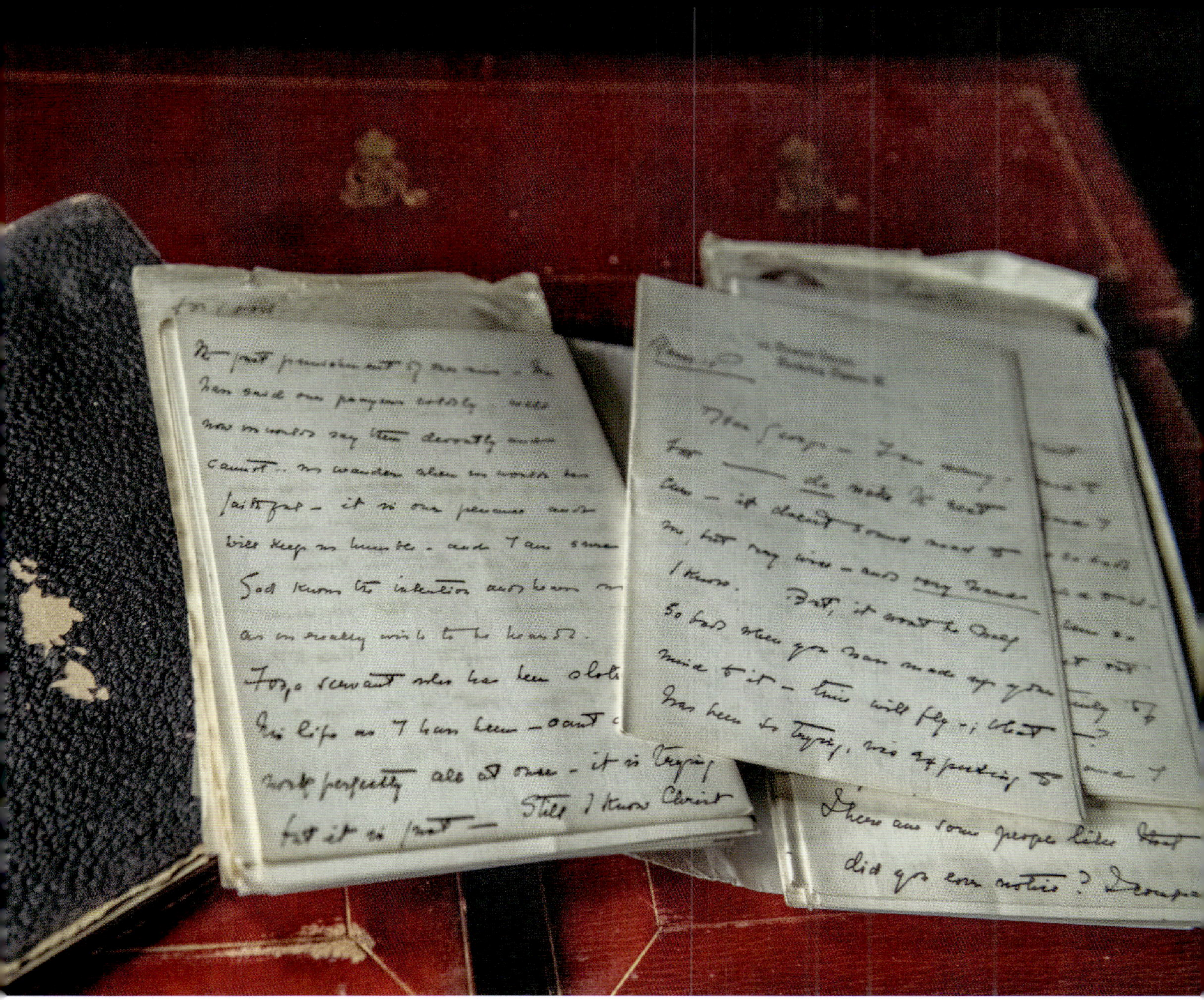

Handwritten letters, journals and diaries of Alberta, Countess of Sandwich, from the family archive.

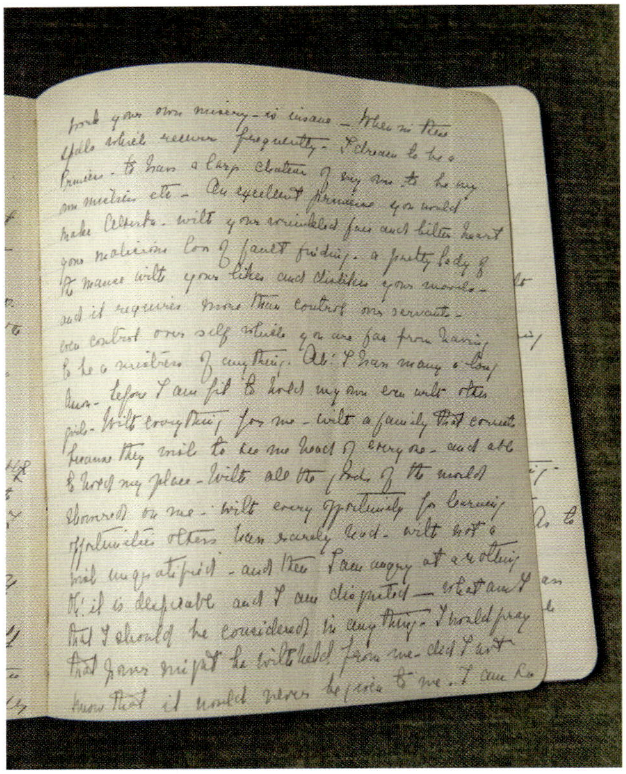

Journal entries from 1899 to 1900, written in Alberta's hand.

are both a challenge and a treasure. Each page is a conversation with the past, revealing a woman who was deeply engaged with her family, her friends and her own inner world.

Reading Alberta's letters is like piecing together a mosaic. She wrote regularly to her mother, Betty, her Aunt Josephine (affectionately known as Aunt Joe), her brother Hollister and to spiritual mentors like Swami Vivekananda. Many letters bore a simple but crucial instruction: 'Please return.' This request, written in pencil, speaks volumes about Alberta's instinct for preservation. It is thanks to her foresight that we now have an unparalleled collection of personal correspondence from a Gilded Age heiress – a rarity among her contemporaries.

While many of these women were remembered through photographs, society gossip or the grandeur of their homes, Alberta gave us something far more valuable: her unfiltered thoughts, feelings and reflections. These letters offer insight into the inner life of a woman navigating two very different worlds, and in doing so, they expand our understanding of the Gilded Age itself – not just as a time of wealth and glamour, but as a period of complex personal evolution, especially for women like Alberta who bridged cultures and expectations.

Some letters and diary entries pulse with emotional vulnerability. In one entry, she writes, 'For four months ago today when Mother returned from California, I have been in one long struggle with myself. I have cried nearly every night . . . In my saner moments I pray for more and more misery for I am learning such invaluable lessons.' In another, she reflects on her spiritual ambitions: 'I feel as if the life now were a preparation for some great role I must play – *qui vivra verra* [time will tell].'

There are moments of self-loathing too. She once noted in her diary in 1899, aged twenty-one, 'I dream of being a princess – to have a large chateau of my own, to be my own mistress etc. An excellent princess you would make Alberta, with your wrinkled face and bitter heart, your malicious love of fault-finding.'

The transcription of these letters, diaries and journals has been a monumental task, made possible by a team of volunteers from the USA, Canada and the UK, together known as the Alberta Research Project. Each letter scanned in the Muniment Room travels across the globe in digital form before returning, transcribed and ready to join our growing digital library. This collaborative effort has not only preserved her words but also created a vibrant community of history enthusiasts who are as invested in her story as I am.

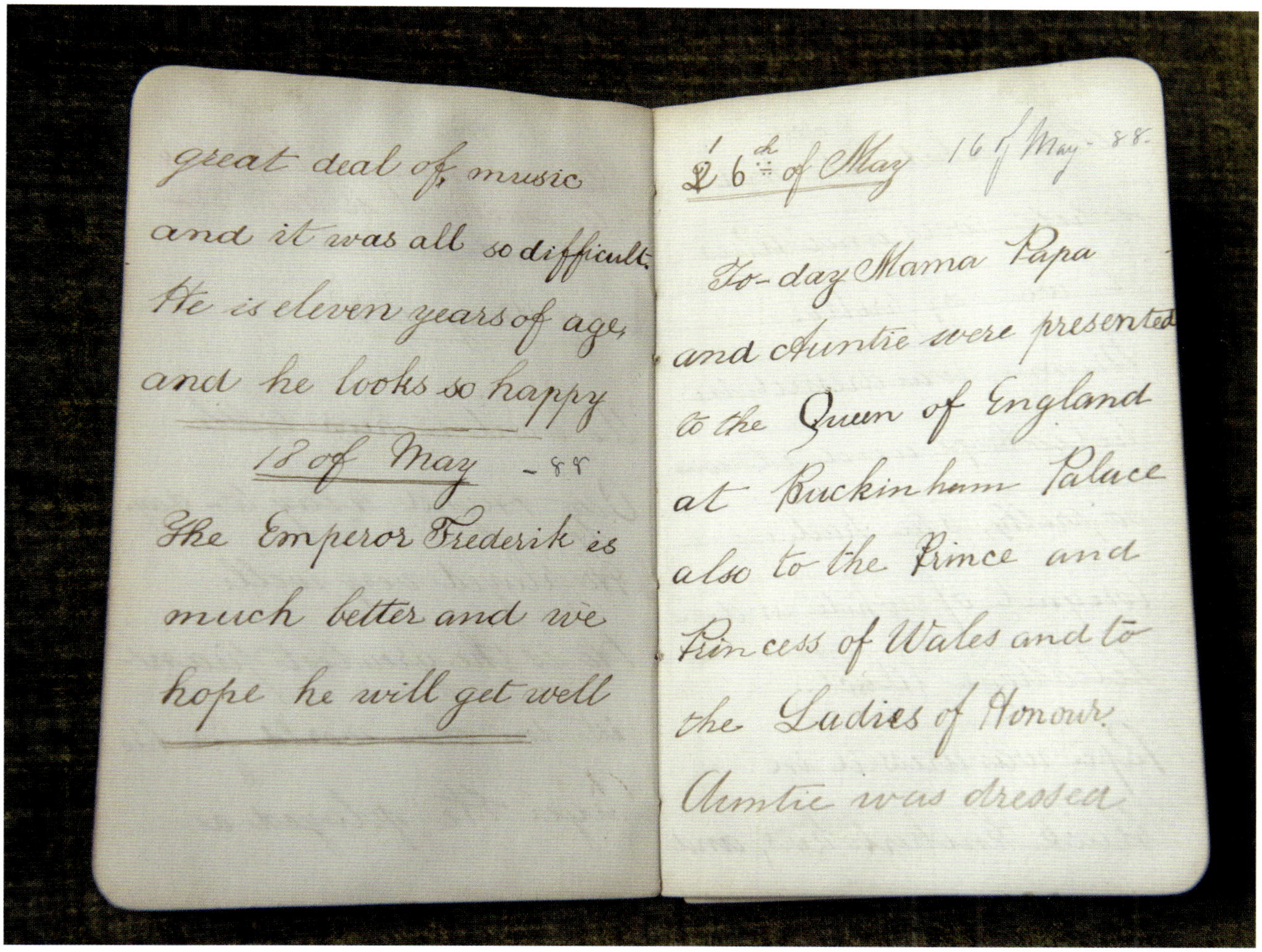

great deal of music
and it was all so difficult.
He is eleven years of age,
and he looks so happy

18 of May -88

The Emperor Frederik is
much better and we
hope he will get well

26th of May 16 of May -88.

To-day Mama Papa
and Auntie were presented
to the Queen of England
at Buckinham Palace
also to the Prince and
Princess of Wales and to
the Ladies of Honour.
Auntie was dressed

Journal entry from 16 May, 1888 when her parents and Aunt were presented to the Queen of England.

Because we now have such an extraordinary volume of material, Luke was able to create something I never imagined possible: the Alberta AI. By uploading her letters into an artificial intelligence platform and doing some tech wizardry, he has essentially allowed Alberta to speak again – in her own words. Visitors can now ask her questions and receive responses directly drawn from her correspondence. Sometimes I catch myself asking how she coped with the British aristocracy, whether she missed home, or how she managed to bridge the cultural divide between America and England – and she answers. Always in her own voice, always with honesty. It's one of the most extraordinary ways I've ever connected with the past.

Among the discoveries in the archives was Alberta's cookbook, a charming selection of recipes she collected and typed, a skill she embraced with enthusiasm. The cookbook is a testament to her domestic life at Hinchingbrooke, where she lived after marrying George Montagu. Its pages offer a glimpse into the kitchens of the past, with recipes and remedies both practical and extravagant, many without measurements – just a

ABOVE Alberta's Book of Receipts, a personal record of household recipes. FACING (*top left*) A copper pot bearing the Sandwich family mark. (*top right and bottom*) Cooking Alberta's recipes.

AGA

pinch of this and a dash of that.

For example, her *Canards aux Cerises* begins, 'Roast a duck, wild or tame, and see to its being rather underdone,' before calling for a sauce of preserved cherries (never in brandy), a spoonful of brown sauce and the duck's own gravy, all gently heated 'without letting it boil'.

Her *Tomates Farcies* instructs the cook to empty and wash large tomatoes, then fill them with a savoury mixture of butter, onion, fennel and rice, all cooked in salt water until 'thoroughly done & dry'. They are then dressed and finished with oil in a sharp oven.

And the *Mousse de Chocolat* is a standout – rich yet airy. It reads, 'For 6 persons, place 2 tablets of a slab of chocolate in a stewpan. Heat this until it is soft, then break it up with a spoon and work in slowly a large half pint of hot water . . . add whipped cream & a trifle of powdered sugar.'

These dishes now feature in our American Heiress Suppers, part of the Grand Historic Tours we host at Mapperton (see page 135). Guests dine by candlelight as Alberta's world comes to life through food, storytelling and the quiet elegance of the house. Her recipes, drawing on both American flair and Continental technique, would have delighted British guests with their rich flavours and charming unfamiliarity.

The Muniment Room, the Alberta Research Project, and the countless letters that continue to be transcribed are all part of the legacy she left behind. In many ways, Alberta was an archivist of her own life, a woman who understood the importance of preserving her experiences for future generations. It is a privilege to continue that work, to share her story and to ensure that her voice is heard.

Through her letters, Alberta offers us a clear and detailed record of a life that bridged two worlds – American and British, spiritual and social. She was reflective, determined and deeply curious. Thanks to her careful preservation and the continued efforts of the Alberta Research Project, we can now better understand not only who she was, but how she thought, felt and lived.

FACING Alberta's *Tomates Farcies*.
OVERLEAF The Sandwich coat of arms engraved on silver place settings, laid for dinner in the Dining Room.

Alberta's Legacy in Objects

REDISCOVERING ALBERTA STURGES'S life has been a journey of uncovering not only her letters and diaries, but also the few precious objects she left behind. Historic houses often guard their stories in attics, drawers and trunks long unopened, and Mapperton is no exception. While many of Alberta's belongings have been dispersed over the decades – passed down through generations, gifted to friends or lost altogether – a handful of remarkable pieces remain. They now form the emotional and historical core of the Alberta collection at Mapperton: her portrait by Ambrose McEvoy, the coronation robes and coronets, a small devotional book that bears her engraved name and, most recently, the discovery of a lifetime.

Each piece offers a unique perspective on her life, but this newly discovered book, titled *Sursum Corda* – Latin for 'Lift up your hearts' – gives the most intimate insight. When I first held it, I was caught off guard by its scale. It was so small, as though it was never meant to be seen, only held close. The book is filled with scripture, poetry, prayers, pressed flowers, handwritten notes and clippings that span decades. It seems to have accompanied her through much of her adult life.

Some entries are deeply personal. 'Friends who, in 1905, promised to spend the first of every month in grateful prayer,' she wrote, listing the names of those dearest to her: her children – Victor, Drogo, Faith and Betts. The pages are dotted with dried leaves and flowers. Tucked between the leaves is a clipping marking the birth of my father-in-law: 'A son for Lord Hinchingbrooke'. Another marks the death of Adeline, Duchess of Bedford, in 1920. And on one page, beside the name Alberta she has written simply: 'My godchild'. It's a reference to the daughter of her dear friend Paul Compton. Alberta had grown close to Paul as a young girl, and he had named his child after her. Paul's entire family perished in the sinking of the *Lusitania* in 1915. Alberta's reference to it is subdued, almost reverent. There's no drama on the page – just quiet grief and memory.

The book is part devotional, part diary and part memorial, and as the entries progress through the years, her handwriting grows less steady. But even in the final pages, her voice remains poetic. The last entry is not hers, but her daughter Betts's: 'Mother died peacefully at 11am on Tuesday, October 23, 1951, in the cottage, Hinchingbrooke.' A quiet closing to a life lived with reflection, discipline and love.

We don't yet know exactly when she began her record. Some entries date back to 1901, possibly earlier, and others stretch through the 1930s and 1940s. She clearly kept it close. Today, it's one of the most fragile and powerful items in the collection. The dried flowers are brittle. The paper thinning. But its importance is

Alberta, Countess of Sandwich, on her wedding day, July 25, 1905.

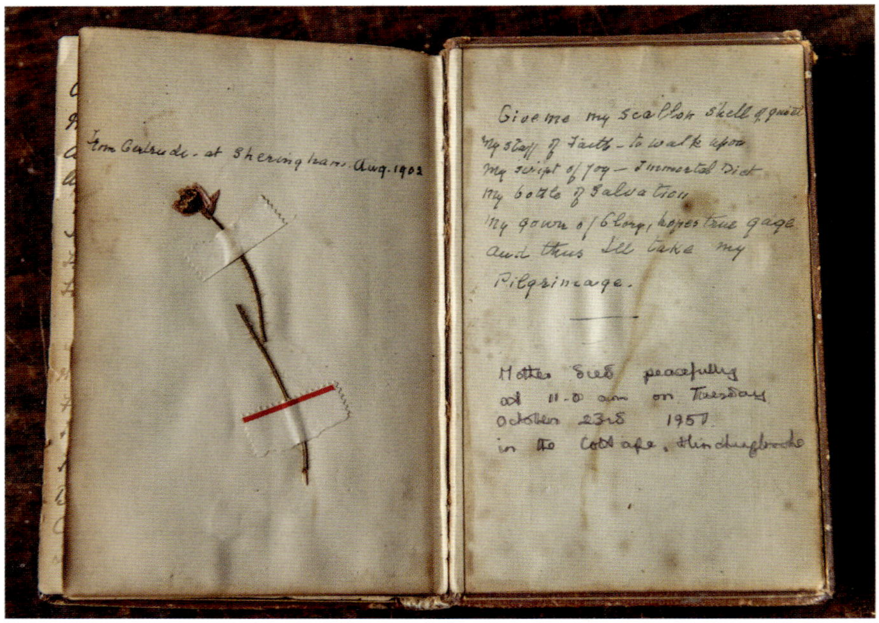

undeniable. It doesn't merely describe Alberta's faith; it carries it. Her spiritual life – like her handwriting – is pressed into every page.

Her visual legacy is no less compelling. One of my favourite paintings in the collection is her portrait by the artist Ambrose McEvoy. Produced at the height of his career, McEvoy was one of the leading portraitists of the early twentieth century, celebrated for his expressive brushwork, tonal daring and the emotional resonance he drew from his sitters. He painted many of society's most admired figures – Consuelo, Duchess of Marlborough, Lady Diana Manners (Cooper), Nancy Cunard – and was known for his ability to capture not just the likeness but the personality of a person.

Alberta's portrait, which now hangs in Mapperton's Staircase Hall, was created during a period when she was navigating her public role as Countess of Sandwich and her more interior, spiritual pursuits. Her gaze in the portrait is steady, reflective, touched by something unknowable. She is both present and apart.

McEvoy himself seems to have felt the power of the collaboration. In one letter to Alberta, he wrote: 'I have been feeling so happy about this portrait. I really feel it is a great success from my point of view and I can never thank you enough for all this help you have given me in painting it.' And after visiting Hinchingbrooke, where he painted in residence, he added: 'I enjoyed my visit to Hinchingbrooke enormously. It is wonderfully stimulating to a painter I think.'

And there was more. McEvoy also painted a group portrait of her three eldest children: Victor, Drogo and Faith. That work was exhibited at the Grosvenor Gallery in London. The painting, McEvoy told Alberta, had been 'a great success', and he noted its broader impact: 'So many people want me to paint groups now.' Tragically, that group portrait was lost in the 1999 fire. But we do have photographs. Black-and-white, slightly faded, but still luminous. One shows McEvoy mid-brushstroke.

Another discovery, equally powerful, came in the lead-up to the coronation of King Charles III in May 2023. I had always suspected that George and Alberta's

ABOVE Alberta's tiny devotional book, *Sursum Corda* ('Lift up your hearts'), filled with prayers, pressed flowers and private notes gathered across a lifetime. FACING Portrait of Alberta, Countess of Sandwich, by Ambrose McEvoy.

coronation outfits still existed, but their exact location remained a mystery. Then they emerged from a storage chest after some persistent digging: the earl's crimson velvet robe and waistcoat, and two coronets – one for the earl and one, smaller and more delicate, for the countess.

The items were in a quite a state. There was staining and tearing, and some of the ermine trim had begun to disintegrate. The coronets, once gleaming with pageantry, had lost their lustre. Just as I had done with Alberta's letters and diaries, I launched a conservation effort to preserve these pieces for the future. With immense thanks to the supporters who contributed to the fundraiser, the items were entrusted to the Royal School of Needlework at Hampton Court Palace.

The RSN's conservators were extraordinary. I visited them twice during the process and was deeply moved by the care and craftsmanship on display. These were not just ceremonial objects; they were markers of history, carried by a woman I had come to know so well.

The robes and coronets were worn at the coronation of King George VI and Queen Elizabeth in May 1937. Alberta recorded the events in her diary. In December 1936, she noted the abdication of Edward VIII. Just five months later, she and George took their places in Westminster Abbey, seated three rows behind the King.

Today, the restored robes and coronets are stored safely in a custom textile box, awaiting their next ceremonial appearance – whenever that may be.

LEFT The Countess coronet and coronation robes, following conservation at the Royal School of Needlework. FACING Painting of Alberta's children by Ambrose McEvoy in 1919 once hung in the Staircase Hall at Mapperton.

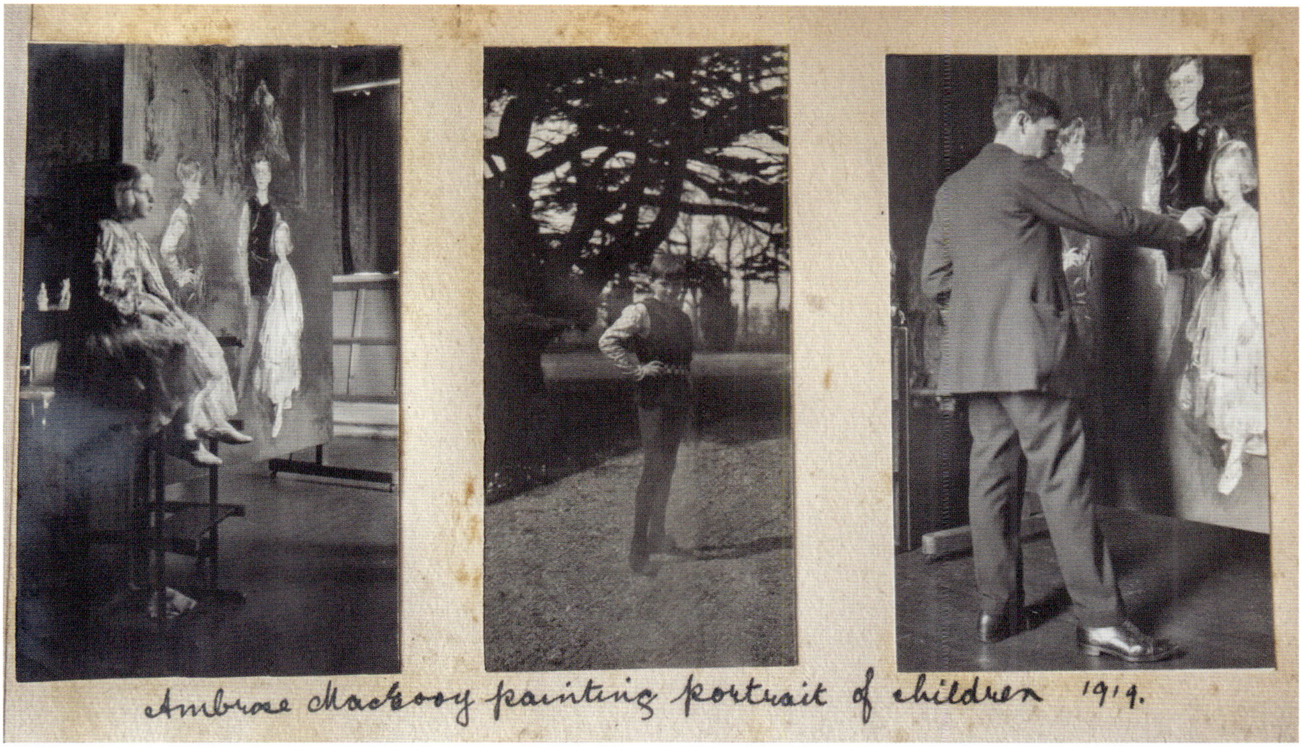
Ambrose MacEvoy painting portrait of children 1919.

THE WORTH DRESS: A TEARFUL DISCOVERY

While writing this book, I experienced what may have been the most emotional discovery of all. After attending the House of Worth exhibition at the Petit Palais in Paris, I returned to Mapperton buzzing. I knew from an old inventory that Alberta had a 1914 dress made by Worth – the prestigious Parisian fashion house founded by Charles Frederick Worth. But despite searching, we hadn't been able to locate it.

Three days after my return from Paris, I was once again rummaging through a trunk, this one filled with old seventeenth-century armour. At the bottom was a bundle of old textiles. I gently pulled them out, unfolded them, and there it was. On the waistband was the label: 'C. Worth'. I burst into tears. It was Alberta's 1914 Worth gown.

The dress is breathtaking. Made of black and gold brocaded chinoiserie satin, it features a high waistline and a gold lamé bodice, with a black satin crossover fastening to one side. The tulle sleeves are delicately weighted with glass beads, and the skirt is adorned with vertical panels of gold and black satin, both front and back. Inside, a wide elasticated waistband bears the iconic woven satin Worth label. The brocade – a fine example of *point rentré* – shimmers as the light catches it. It is now the crown jewel of our Alberta collection.

To hold the past in your hands is a rare gift. To give it voice again is an honour. Alberta's collection reminds us that history isn't always found in grand monuments or public legacies. Sometimes, it waits in the folds of a gown, the brushstrokes of a portrait, the ink of a handwritten letter – waiting to be heard, waiting to be loved back into life.

ABOVE (*top*) A close detail of the extraordinary black and gold brocade, woven in an elaborate chinoiserie design. (*bottom*) The iconic House of Worth label stitched inside the waistband. FACING Alberta's 1914 Worth gown displayed for the first time after its extraordinary rediscovery at Mapperton.

Blenheim and the Duchess Who Left

BLENHEIM PALACE IS ONE of the grandest country houses in Britain, and arguably one of the most politically significant. Built in the early eighteenth century as a gift to John Churchill, the 1st Duke of Marlborough, for his victory at the Battle of Blenheim, it's the only non-royal, non-episcopal residence in England to hold the title of palace. Designed by Sir John Vanbrugh, Blenheim is all drama – monumental architecture, vast courtyards, soaring ceilings and, of course, a sweeping park laid out by 'Capability' Brown. From the beginning, it was meant to symbolize triumph, power and permanence. But like so many great houses, behind its splendour are the complicated lives of those who lived there.

I've always had a quiet fascination with the stories of American heiresses who crossed the Atlantic – women who left behind their own country's dynamism and stepped into the ancient rituals, expectations and constraints of the British aristocracy. As an American – if not an heiress – that interest is, I suppose, personal too. There's something about these transatlantic lives that continues to speak to me.

During the months I was reading Alberta's letters and diaries and tracing the arc of her extraordinary inner life, I came across a letter she wrote to her Aunt Josephine, dated 30 November 1906. It offers a fascinating glimpse into the unravelling of another American heiress's story: that of Consuelo Vanderbilt, 9th Duchess of Marlborough.

I'd already known something of Consuelo's life – her empty and oppressive marriage, the grandeur of Blenheim Palace, the deep unhappiness behind all the pomp – but here, in Alberta's own hand, was a contemporary, personal account of that very moment when it all began to fall apart:

> The King has absolutely refused to receive the Duke of Marlborough at court. Lady Lansdowne too will not receive him. Lady Randolph Churchill too has launched a cold shoulder. Winston Churchill is hand-to-hand with the Duke, consequently I suppose the rest of society is down upon her too. Except the Princess Christian who doesn't believe a word of the story. Du[chess] Adeline is seeing a good deal of her – likes her, feels desperately sorry … she, Consuelo, doesn't deny anything – it is hard, very – for she has wonderful qualities. Oh! I am so disappointed about it. The whole affair is so mismanaged. No? Vanderbilt went to America and the same day Hon. Belmont arrived and is installed there. There is nothing like one's own sweet house – it's long peace, joy and strength unspeakable.

Blenheim Palace.

It's a remarkable letter – full of sympathy, dismay and a kind of woman-to-woman recognition. Alberta wasn't writing for history. She was writing from the heart, from the vantage point of someone who, like Consuelo, had crossed the ocean and entered a world shaped by codes and silences.

Later, I had the opportunity to visit Blenheim Palace myself while filming for my American Countess YouTube channel. And as I walked through those towering halls and endless galleries, I couldn't help but think of that letter. Blenheim is extraordinary – grand beyond comprehension – but it's also a place that can easily swallow you up.

What struck me most that day wasn't just the history of Churchill or the monumentality of Vanbrugh's architecture. It was the image of Consuelo with her husband and two sons painted by John Singer Sargent – an American artist capturing an American heiress – poised and standing in that vast palace that had become both her stage and her prison. The portrait is exquisite – luminous and restrained – but knowing what came next, it's almost unbearable in its quietness.

Consuelo married the 9th Duke in 1895, pushed into the match by her ambitious mother, Alva Vanderbilt, who saw the British aristocracy as the ultimate prize. The marriage gave the Marlboroughs the money they needed to restore Blenheim; it gave Consuelo a title and a role. But it didn't give her happiness. Eventually, she left.

Alberta's phrase – 'There is nothing like one's own sweet house – it's long peace, joy and strength unspeakable' – says so much. It's not just a commentary on Consuelo's departure. It's a declaration of what truly matters. Alberta had begun to understand, perhaps more than most, that beauty and scale mean nothing without peace. That no palace – no title – is worth the cost of yourself.

And perhaps that's why these stories continue to matter to me. Not because of the gowns or the grandeur, but because of what these women carried. Their decisions. Their strength. Their disappointments. Their longing for a place to simply be themselves.

Blenheim remains one of the greatest houses in the country – staggering in scale and rich in symbolism. Today it's visited by thousands each year, drawn by its grandeur, its history and the stories embedded in its walls. And yet, for all its public presence, it still holds the echo of private lives once endured within it – lives like Consuelo's. Perhaps that's the real legacy of these great houses: not just the architecture or the lineage, but the tension between public display and private reality. Between what we preserve and what we remember.

Singer Sargent portrait of Consuelo Vanderbilt and her son Lord Ivor Spencer-Churchill.

Index

PICTURE CREDITS

COVER IMAGES
Front cover: © Jessica Fulford-Dobson
Back cover, left: © Beth Davis
Back cover, middle and right:
© Jessica Fulford-Dobson

INTERIOR IMAGES
All images © Jessica Fulford-Dobson,
except for the following:

Pages 2, 91, 134
Chris Atkins

Pages 6–7, 12, 15, 18, 46, 242–3
© Mapperton Estate

Pages 48–9, 68, 70, 75, 100–1, 199, 205, 250
© Beth Davis

Page 59
Watershed PR

Pages 60, 62, 63, 64, 108, 110, 111, 158,
160, 161, 162–3, 212, 214, 215, 216–7
© Sam Rose

Page 77
Mike Holden/Alamy

Pages 94, 96 (top left), 142–3, 188,
190–1, 200, 234
© Julie Montagu

Page 129
The National Trust Photolibrary/Alamy

Page 131
scenicireland.com/Christopher Hill
Photographic/Alamy

Page 179
Robert Christopher/Alamy

Page 181
GL Archive/Alamy

Page 198 (top left)
Graham Mellanby

Page 237
© Phil Barker/Country Life Picture Library

Page 239
Robert Wyatt/Alamy

Page 240
Francis G. Mayer/Corbis/VCG via
Getty Images

Page 253
© Millie Pilkington / Country Life Magazine

MAPPERTON

Beaminster,
Dorset,
DT8 3NR

mapperton.com

Visiting Times: Mapperton House, Gardens & Wildlands are typically open from beginning of March to end of October. Mapperton is closed on Fridays and Saturdays (except for special events).

BOUGHTON HOUSE

Geddington Road,
Kettering,
Northamptonshire,
NN14 1BJ

www.boughtonhouse.co.uk

Visiting Times: Boughton opens on selected dates in the spring and summer.

Boughton Gardens and Parkland are usually open for several brief periods throughout the year: February, late March/April, late May bank holiday, August, October and December.

CASTLE COOLE

Enniskillen,
County Fermanagh,
Northern Ireland,
BT74 6JY

nationaltrust.org.uk/visit/northern-ireland/castle-coole

Visiting Times: The house is available to see by guided tour only from March-October.

MEDMENHAM ABBEY AND THE HELLFIRE CAVES

The abbey is a private residence and is not open to the public; see below for information about the Hellfire Caves.

Church Lane,
West Wycombe,
HP14 3AH

hellfirecaves.co.uk

Visiting Times: Check the website.

BLENHEIM PALACE

Woodstock,
Oxfordshire,
OX20 1UL

blenheimpalace.com

Visiting Times: Open daily, except on 25 December.

ACKNOWLEDGEMENTS

THERE ARE MANY PEOPLE BEHIND THE making of this book, and it feels only right to begin with those who have helped shape how Mapperton will be seen within these pages.

Malcolm Winyard – stylist, interior designer extraordinaire and dear friend – was there from the very beginning, when I first asked: 'Shall we make this book together?' He brought his beady little eye to the interiors, instinctively understanding how to capture the spirit of a house that has evolved over centuries. Alongside him, Jessica Fulford-Dobson, our principal photographer and a close family friend, approached Mapperton with both artistry and a deep understanding of it as a lived-in home. From those first conversations, the three of us became a dream team – working through everything together and bringing this book to life.

A special gratitude goes to my in-laws, John and Caroline, whose determination safeguarded this house through decades when its future could so easily have been otherwise.

The Mapperton team and our wonderful volunteers are the heart of this place. Day in and day out, through every season, they bring life, care and energy to the estate. Thank you.

To Alice Graham, Editorial Director at Frances Lincoln – thank you for first approaching me with this idea and for believing in it from the very beginning. Your encouragement, and your patience with my very delayed emails and deadlines, were instrumental in bringing this project into being. And to Róisín Duffy, Editor at Frances Lincoln, who worked tirelessly through hundreds of photographs and the layout of these pages, shaping how the book would ultimately come together – I am enormously grateful.

And finally, to my own family. To Luke, who has supported me in ways both visible and invisible, and to our four children – Emma, Jack, William and Nestor – who have watched me take this on and, quite reasonably, wondered how it was possible to add one more thing to my plate. Your quiet encouragement has helped me across the finish line.

This book, like Mapperton itself, is the result of many hands, much care and an enduring belief that these places – and their stories – matter.

ABOUT THE AUTHOR

JULIE MONTAGU, COUNTESS OF SANDWICH, is not your average aristocrat. Born on the outskirts of Chicago, she describes herself as an all-American girl who unexpectedly met the future Earl of Sandwich and then married into the British aristocracy.

Two decades later, Julie is the driving force behind Mapperton House, Gardens & Wildlands in Dorset, where Mapperton House is widely regarded as one of England's finest manor houses. She shares her daily life at Mapperton with a global audience through the Mapperton Live! YouTube channel, alongside her husband Luke. Her Facebook and Instagram platforms have hundreds of thousands of followers, and her continued research in the Montagu family archives has made her an instant Substack bestseller.

Alongside managing the estate, Julie has built a successful career as a wellness entrepreneur and yoga instructor, writing several bestselling books and appearing on Bravo's *Ladies of London*. As a historian, she is a sought-after presenter and commentator on British history and royal affairs for both UK and US networks. In 2020, she presented *An American Aristocrat's Guide to Great Estates* for the Smithsonian Channel. She later launched the American Countess YouTube channel, where her production company, Living History Films, produces high-quality documentaries exploring Britain's stately homes. In 2026, she founded The Countess of Sandwich Society, an independent, member-funded initiative dedicated to archiving, documenting and conserving Britain's historic homes and estates for future generations.

Quarto

First published in 2026 by Frances Lincoln,
an imprint of The Quarto Group.
One Triptych Place, London, SE1 9SH,
United Kingdom
T (0)20 7700 9000
www.Quarto.com

EEA Representation, WTS Tax d.o.o., Žanova ulica 3,
4000 Kranj, Slovenia
www.wts-tax.si

A catalogue record for this book is available from the British Library.

ISBN 978-1-83600-728-9
EBOOK ISBN 978-1-83600-729-6

10 9 8 7 6 5 4 3 2 1

Design by DSGN Dept.

Editorial Director: Alice Graham
Managing Editor: Laura Bulbeck
Editor: Róisín Duffy
Senior Designer: Isabel Eeles
Senior Production Controller: Rohana Yusof
Stylist: Malcolm Winyard

Printed in Guangdong, China TT062026

MIX
Paper | Supporting
responsible forestry
FSC® C016973